"In the 17th Century, Alexis de Tocqueville predicted that America would eventually degenerate into an all-controlling government or aristocracy. In *The Coming Aristocracy*, Oliver DeMille warns in a crystal clear and no-nonsense style that Tocqueville's prediction is rapidly becoming a reality. DeMille outlines the probable American leadership and social structure for the next twenty to thirty years, along with the political construct and methods used by prominent behind-the-scenes players to strengthen and maintain their power. He discusses the fall of freedom and the resulting adverse effects. And he pulls no punches when he describes how to reverse this liberty-destroying agenda. *The Coming Aristocracy* is a virtual treasure map where DeMille's 'X' does mark the spot and the treasure is a life of liberty for our posterity."

> — **Dr. Shanon Brooks**,
> FOUNDER, FACE TO FACE WITH GREATNESS SEMINARS, INC.

"At long last — *real* solutions in the battle for freedom. *The Coming Aristocracy* boils down complexity to core principles to provide a refreshing, insightful, comprehensive, and ultimately inspiring handbook for solving America's cultural, political, and economic problems. Its core strength is that it empowers ordinary individuals to play an integral role in the process. Discouragement and inaction can be readily discarded by following the liberating and detailed path laid out by Oliver DeMille."

> — **Stephen Palmer**,
> CO-FOUNDER, KGAPS CONSULTING

"Oliver DeMille has uncommon vision that he has gained from a deliberate and careful process of reading, observing, dialoguing, distilling, re-reading, pondering, teaching and finally synthesizing critical trends into concise, lucid, and compelling calls to action. *The Coming Aristocracy* is a call that must be heeded if we are to secure freedom and prosperity for ourselves and our children."

> — **David Grant**,
> DEPARTMENT OF BUSINESS, SOUTHERN UTAH UNIVERSITY;
> FOUNDER & VICE PRESIDENT, METALCRAFT PRECISION PRODUCTS, LLC

The Coming Aristocracy

EDUCATION AND THE FUTURE OF FREEDOM

Oliver DeMille

The Center for
SOCIAL LEADERSHIP

The Coming Aristocracy
Education and the Future of Freedom
Oliver DeMille

Copyright © 2009 Oliver DeMille
All rights reserved.
First printing, July 2009. Second printing, July 2011.

Published and Distributed by The Center for Social Leadership
www.thesocialleader.com

For ordering information and bulk discounts, send an email to info@thesocialleader.com, or visit www.thecomingaristocracy.com.

Design and composition by www.danielruesch.com
Cover illustration and design by www.danielruesch.com

DeMille, Oliver
The Coming Aristocracy: Education and the Future of Freedom

ISBN: 978-0-9830996-4-2

Table of Contents

Acknowledgements

I would like to thank Daniela Larsen
for suggesting this work,
and Stephen Palmer for his help.

Many others provided ideas,
research support and other aid—
thank you all.

To Virgil,

whose verses warned free Romans
that an empire was coming.

They should have listened.

"The year was 2081, and everybody was finally equal. They weren't only equal before God and the law. They were equal every which way. Nobody was smarter than anybody else. Nobody was better looking than anybody else. Nobody was stronger or quicker than anybody else. All this equality was due to the 211th, 212th, and 213th Amendments to the Constitution, and to the unceasing vigilance of agents of the United States Handicapper General."

—*Kurt Vonnegut*

"Today's learner will have 10-14 jobs by the age of 38."

—*U.S. Department of Labor*

Aristocracy vs. Freedom

What will our great-grandchildren inherit,
and how will we explain it to them?

A new era is upon us. Many in the New Age movement believe that an Aquarian wisdom, equality, and prosperity for all are just ahead. The more down-to-earth, "left-brained" (or "unenlightened") among us see this as unfounded, but struggle to explain and especially solve the economic, political, and societal crises we face. A religious right sees economic downturn and the threat of worse ahead as fulfillment of prophecy and a natural result of modern immorality, while futurists, trend analysts, and scenario planners remove constants from their formulas and boldly predict…change.

This author has no crystal ball to see what's ahead. Perhaps the best forecast so far has been Strauss and Howe's *The Fourth Turning*, which projected that these crises were just around the corner and put into print very 9/11-like and economic crises predictions before they were generally evident. Based on their research and his own, Harry S. Dent has provided astoundingly accurate stock market predictions. But this book isn't an outline for the future of our society in general.

This book does address one emergent reality in the world—the return of aristocratic rule in the United States. While this trend is not limited to North America (indeed it may well be *the* challenge to every nation in the 21st century), it was the fledgling United States that first and most definitively put the ruling aristocratic class out of power for nearly two centuries.

Of course, aristocracy still existed—but its monopoly on power was busted. And it lasted!

For the United States to now fall back under the lash of aristocratic rule is a tragedy greater than any penned by Shakespeare, and it signals to the rest of the world that the era of freedom is limited; change is upon us.

There are many battlefields where aristocracy and freedom clash—from government and economy to media, family, immigration, community, entertainment, business, finance, religion, art, travel, law, investment, construction, technology, design, and the list goes on. But nowhere is the battle greater than in education. I speak here not of schools, budgets, educational laws, legislatures, administrations, or curricula—few of these have much to do with *learning* anyway. But the learning a student obtains—or does not obtain—will in large part determine his or her future. Please note the word "learning"—not degree, credential, graduation, or school.

Class status in the future *may* be influenced by degrees, credentials and/or prestige, but it will *certainly* be determined by learning—or its lack.

More importantly, in a society that worships financial success above everything else, the greatest danger is that we'll only have three types of people: aristocrats, their agents and employees, and dependents.

The other type of individual and family has been called many things—*yeomen* in British history, *frontiersmen, cowboys,* or *mavericks* in American lore, and also *pioneers, adventurers, landowners,* and *shopkeepers.*

More recent terms include *entrepreneurs* (including *social entrepreneurs*), *leaders* (including *social leaders*), *disruptive innovators, outliers,* and *anomalies.* Americans tend to wear such labels with pride. It is an interesting linguistical question to consider if perhaps the American English is more replete with such terms than the British nomenclature, and if such terms are considered derogatory. It is, after all, what the Revolution was about: Either live to work for aristocrats, or live to build for oneself and one's posterity. And if the British tended to look down on such cheekiness, other European and Asian nations had few positive names for such people—if they had any at all.

It was not always so. Before the "civilization" of Europe, when clans and tribes prevailed, the term "frank" (meaning "free man") was so culturally significant that its derivatives are still found representing the currency of several nations and the very name of France, its language and its people.

In spite of, or rather because of, the aristocratic paternalism that existed in Georgian England, Jefferson was a proponent of a nation of *independents*—owners of their own farms, shops or trade, and the idea that such independents would keep America free. Hamilton argued that a nation of *dependents*—people working as employees for others—would make a better America, with more wealth in a ruling class. He had previously taken the opposite position while helping to write *The Federalist Papers*, but he subsequently felt an aristocracy would be needed to successfully compete with, and remain independent of, Europe. Of course, history reflects that the majority of Americans favored Jefferson's approach, and an idealistic system free of upper-class rule was established. The American founders created an educational model that purposed to bring up all youth with aristocratic education, and their "classless" model lasted longer than any other in written history.

Today we live in a different system: an aristocracy. There are, in our aristocracy, the following types of people:

- Aristocrats

- Their agents

- Employees of the agents

- Non-employee dependents

- Owners

It is upon this last group—the owners—that America was built and became great. If it is to become great again, two things must happen: 1) The owners must again lead, and 2) a significant number of the citizens must again become owners. This is a matter of education, pure and simple—but not necessarily *formal* education. The learning must occur, however, or we will pass on to our children an aristocracy, where no one—not even the rulers—is free.

So, to state it succinctly: Our generation will either create an aristocracy or freedom. This book is about this battle, and how freedom can win. Today, freedom is desperately disadvantaged. It will take several miracles for freedom to triumph, the most important one being the "mini-factory" revolution, which I outline in the next chapter.

To facilitate just such miracles is the other objective of this book. Many of these "miracles" were born into your homes in recent years—or soon will be. This book is dedicated to the parents who embrace the long-term reality of allowing these miracles the additional miracle of a superb, world-class leadership education.

Either aristocracy or freedom will win the world in the years ahead. So this is very personal! Which side are you on? Which side were your children born to support and engage? Will you help them?

Our grandchildren will live their lives within the context and ramifications of this choice—free, or stuck in whatever level of an aristocracy (and all levels are lamentable) they inherit or achieve. While the message of fear is to "get ahead" in aristocratic terms, the call of leadership is to help build a world that is free. The era of aristocracy is coming…unless a new generation of leaders arises.

Look into the eyes of your children, or grandchildren, and ask yourself what is there. Do they seek aristocracy, or freedom? Consider. Then do the same test in the mirror.

These essays are dedicated to the leaders of the 21st Century, who stand for freedom, and who have the courage to make the miracles of freedom a reality.

CHAPTER 1

The Solution: Mini-Factories

Freedom, you were everything.

I f freedom is to reverse the onslaught of American and global aristocracy, it will likely do so through the greatest freedom trend of our time. This trend is revolutionizing institutions, organizations, relationships, society and even nations around the world. It is still in its infancy, and many have yet to realize its potential. The experts tend to overlook it because it seems small. In fact, it is bigger than any of the trends I list in Chapter 12. However, it will likely always seem small because it is a "bottom-up" trend with no "top-down" organizations, alliances, or even affiliations. Truthfully, it isn't even a single trend at all—it is thousands of small trends, all following a similar pattern.

Malcolm Gladwell called this great trend, or at least part of it, "outliers," Harry S. Dent called it the "customization" explosion, Alvin Toffler said it is the wave of "revolutionary wealth" as led in large part by "prosumers," John Naisbitt named it the "high touch" megatrend, Stephen Covey called it the 8th Habit of "greatness," Daniel Pink coined the descriptor "free agent nation," and Seth Godin refers to it as "tribes." Others have termed it "social entrepreneurship," "the new leadership," "a new age," and even "the human singularity." All of these touch on facets of this freedom trend, but I think the best, most accurate and descriptive name for it is the "mini-factory" model.

Modernism came with the factory—the ability to mass produce. This revolutionized the world—economics, governments, how we spend our time each day, what we eat and wear, relationships, the size and functions of our homes and cities, etc. It changed everything.

Today the mini-factory is changing everything just as drastically. In ancient times the wealthy set up estates or fiefdoms to cover all their needs, and the masses worked to provide the needs of their aristocratic "superiors." In modern times the factory provided mass goods and services.

Imagine the impact on everything in our lives if each family could provide all, or even many, of its needs for itself—and do it better than kings or politicians ruling over working peasants or even corporations employing workers to produce goods and services. Such is the world of the mini-factory.

For example, what if parents could educate their children better than local school factories, with the best teachers, classes and resources of the world piped directly into their own home? What if a sick person had more time and motivation to research the cases of her symptoms than the factory doctors, and the availability of all the latest medical journals right on her computer screen? She would also have holistic works, original studies, alternative and collaborative experts, and the ability to email the experts and get answers in less time than it would take to wait in the hospital lobby. Ten friends would likely send her their experiences with similar illness within days of her mentioning casually online that she was sick. If she chose a certain surgeon, a dozen people might share their experiences with this doctor. What if integrative doctors did house calls again?

What if a mother planning to travel for a family vacation could just book flights and hotels herself, without calling the "expert" travel agent? Maybe she could even choose seats on the flight or see pictures of her hotel room—all in her own home between her projects and errands.

Welcome to the world of the mini-factory. I purposely used examples that are already a reality. But they were just a futuristic dream when writers like Alvin Toffler and John Naisbitt predicted them before 1990. Cartoon flip phones made super heroes, and the remote communicators in *Star Trek* seemed centuries away.

But this revolution isn't just about technology. Technology

has helped it, but the impetus of the mini-factory trend is freedom. People want to spend less time at the factory/corporation and more time at home. They want to be more involved in raising their children and improving their love life. In an aristocracy, these luxuries are reserved for the upper class. In a free society, anyone can build a mini-factory.

So what is a mini-factory? A mini-factory is anything someone does—alone or with partners or a team—that accomplishes what has historically (meaning the last 150 years of modernism) been done *en masse* or by big institutions. If a charter school provides better education for some of the community, it's a mini-factory. If it does it at less cost and/or in less time spent in the classroom, so much the better.

A homeschool or private school can be a mini-factory. Of course, if the charter, private, or home school does a worse job than the regular factory, it is a failed mini-factory. If joining a multi-level company and building it into a source of real income serves you better than an employee position, it's a mini-factory. If downsizing from a lucrative professional job in Los Angeles to a private practice or job that pays much less but allows you twice as much time with your family and a more relaxed lifestyle in, say, Flagstaff or Durango and makes you happier, it's a mini-factory. Choose an industry, add the word "alternative" plus a hyphen, and you can make a good stab at a mini-factory option.

Again, a mini-factory is where you do something that has been done historically by institutions, but you do it just as well (or in a way that is preferable for some reason) on a smaller scale. And successful mini-factories get better results than the institutionalized factories. Of course, some things may be done better by the big institutions—and we'll want those to stay around.

If the quaint, wonderful, little local bookstore goes out of business in the face of Amazon or Barnes & Nobel mega-sellers, recreate a bookstore/library by remodeling a room in your house, or cooperate with friends to create a special "reading time" once a week, etc. There are as many possibilities as your creativity and priorities will allow.

Entrepreneurship, alternative education, the downshifter movement, environmental groups, alternative health, the growth of spirituality, community architecture, the explosion of network marketing, home doctor visits, the rebirth of active fathering, and so many other trends are mini-factories. The American Founder's mini-factory was more localized, caring, interactive government. The one-room schoolhouse with its individualized mentoring and education of everyone—regardless of class—was the foundation of classless society. As long as it lasted, so did our democratic freedom.

Gardening was a foundation of American health, and general health has decreased with its diminishment. Big institutions helped eradicate infectious diseases, and today a combination of these advances with the resurgence of family gardening is a mini-factory victory.

Immigrants to the U.S. tend to be the most mini-factory focused group of all, which is why it's interesting to hear that immigration is such a "problem" to the aristocratic establishment.

Another example: Compare martial arts studios to the military. If your goal is hand-to-hand combat training, an excellent martial arts teacher who gives you personal instruction over the course of several years is a much better high-quality plan. Can you imagine what would happen if the government or a huge company set up martial arts studios in all towns and cities and used the same curriculum? More people would have martial arts classes, and a black belt would mean less and less. The quality of learning would decrease.

It all comes down to this: *Big, institutional, non-transparent, bureaucratic organizations are natural supporters of aristocracy. Freedom flourishes when the people are independent, free, and as self-sufficient as possible.*

I am not suggesting going backwards in any way. Forward progress is most likely in a nation that is both well educated and highly trained; where big institutional solutions are offered wherever they are best and individuals and groups seek smaller solutions where they better serve their needs; where free enterprise rules apply and there are no special benefits or perks of class (either conservative aristocracy or liberal meritocracy); and where government, business, family, academia, religion, media, and community all fulfill their distinct, equally-important roles. Such a model is called freedom. It has been the best system for the most people in the history of the world, and it still is.

To adopt freedom in our time, either the aristocracy must give up its perks and voluntarily restructure society, or the masses must retake their freedoms bit by bit, day by day, by establishing mini-factories.

Mini-factories will be more successful if each person only does a few, and does them with true excellence. Freedom will flourish best if there is no organization or even coordination of the mini-factories; if individuals, partners, families and teams identify what is needed in the world and in their own lives and set out to deliver it. This will likely not be popular with or accepted by the experts—until it works, and until it can offer them a job.

This is especially hard in a time like ours where the employee mindset wants someone to "fix" things (like the economy, health care, education, etc.), precisely when an entrepreneurial mindset is most needed to take risks and initiate the best and most lasting changes.

If real, positive and effective change is to come, it will most likely be initiated by the people acting as individuals, small groups, and teams. If it comes from the top it will tend to only bring more aristocracy, and the day of freedom will be over for now.

Whatever your mini-factory contribution might be, consider that it will help determine the future of freedom. Mini-factories can be hard to establish and challenging to build. Many people fail once or several times before they learn to be effective. But the type of learning that only comes from failing and then trying again is the most important in building leaders and citizens who are capable of maintaining freedom in a society. Note that this very type of education is rejected in a training model of schooling, where failure is seen as unacceptable and students are taught to avoid it at all costs. This mindset only works if an aristocracy is there to take care of the failures. In a freedom model, citizens and leaders learn the vital lessons of challenges; failures and wise risk-taking are needed.

Starting and leading a mini-factory, and indeed all entrepreneurial work, is challenging. Those who embraced this difficult path in history established and maintained freedom, while those who embraced the ease of past compromises sold themselves and their posterity into aristocracy. In the long term, though, aristocracy is much harder on everyone than freedom.

There are currently mini-factories in almost every field and nation. As you consider what mini-factories you should support, start and build, just ask what things could be done (or are being done) better by a small mini-factory than by the big organizations that try to manage or control nearly everything in our world. If it could be done just as well by a mini-factory, the change to the smaller entity can drastically promote freedom. If it can be done even better by a mini-factory, it is better for life itself! The mini-factory is the new vehicle of freedom.

Take a mini-survey: What are your pet complaints? Government? Develop family government models. Health Care? Educate yourself on prevention and self-care. Education? Learn the principles of Leadership Education. Media? Start a blog. Entertainment? Develop a group of hobbyists who share your interests, whether it be Harley road trips, ice fishing, scrapbooking, etc.

You get the idea: Live deliberately, and do not wait for institutions to change to meet your needs. Do not waste your energy or good humor on complaining. Find a mini-factory that does it right and get behind it—or start one yourself. So many are needed, and they can bring the miracle of freedom!

The future remains unseen. It is the undiscovered country. Many ancients felt that fate drove the future, but the idea of freedom taught humanity to look each to his/herself, to partner with others, and to take the risk to build community and take action now in order to pass on a better life to our children and our children's children.

Today, that concept of freedom is waning—slowly and surely being replaced by a class culture. Even those who criticize this idea, who claim that there is no growing upper classes and probably won't be, belie their own thesis by doing all they can to make sure their own children get ahead—as close to the top of the socio-economic strata as possible. Those who love freedom, whatever their stripe—be they green, red, blue, rainbow, or anything else—are needed. They need to see what is really happening, and they need to educate themselves adequately to make a difference. The most powerful changes toward freedom will likely be made by mini-factories, in thousands and hopefully millions of varieties and iterations.

Aristocracy or freedom—*the future of the globe*—hangs in the balance....

CHAPTER 2

Freedom Education

The future of freedom depends upon it.

The challenge of aristocratic rule is time. Upper classes think, plan and act generationally, mid-term and short-term. The middle classes think, plan and act mid- and short-term ("retirement," and also "next paycheck"), while the lower classes live paycheck to paycheck, with the occasional payday loan. It is the long-term generational mindset and behavior of the upper class that maintains their rule over other classes.

Most revolutions in history have consisted of short- or mid-term approaches, and they usually fail in less than a decade. The upper class may lose power for a short time, but not in the long-term. This occurs because most revolutions or reforms in society have short or mid-term goals—even those that succeed are not designed to last.

The genius of the American Founding model is that it was a revolution on all three time levels: The U.S. Constitution with its separations, checks and balances created a short-term legal equality of individuals, *regardless* of their class status; the structure of the Senate established a mid-term check on the upper class, which lasted over a century; but the greatest genius was that the non-governmental institutions of family, community, religions, schools, businesses and media were put on the same level as government in terms of power and influence.

The Northwest Ordinance accomplished something new and incredibly effective: Educate everyone (whatever their class, indeed, regardless of class) like the aristocrats of Europe. Specifically, teach every young American to think long-term (generationally), mid-term (decades), and short-term (this year and next).

This type of thinking is not just a matter of putting one's attention to longer time spans. To think in terms of humanity's future, the mind must be introduced to and immersed in humanity's past and long struggle—day in and day out over many years. That's quality aristocratic education, found mostly in histories and the great classics from every field. Likewise, to think effectively in the mid-term, one needs intensive topical training for several years. Both types work best under the guidance of good mentors. Ideally, each person gets both types of education in his or her youth.

This type of education naturally produces leaders who think

broadly and deeply on a variety of topics, and are able to apply breadth- and depth-thinking to any given subject as needed. Moreover, this kind of education produces a person who naturally sees things in the short-, mid- and long-term simultaneously. When access to this type of education is limited to the few by law, by price or by committees of experts, the system is elitist. When such education is available but many middle and lower class youth don't seek it because they don't see its value, we have the epitome of aristocratic society—where the under classes don't even know how, or even seem to desire, to access class mobility and think only in short- or mid-terms. Both of these models exist in our current aristocracy.

What is needed is for "regular" people—citizens from middle and lower classes—to attain the education of mid- and long-term, by doing what the upper classes have always done and still do: Obtain great, mentored education in the greatest works of history, math and science, government and economics, literature and technology, biography and the arts, languages and communication skills, current events and philosophy, etc.

Leadership Education never died. The elites have used it as the key to maintaining their power. In the Information Age, educational quality (defined as the level of one's ability and tendency to think—broadly, deeply, on any new topic, and effectively across all time spans) is the greatest determining factor of prosperity and freedom. The challenge, however, is that in our modern world this education is nearly monopolized by elites and ignored by others.

The solution is Leadership Education for everyone! The future of freedom depends on it. Those who look past the mantra "Education is job training," who see long-term, and who realize that truly quality education will prepare them and their children for leadership will be the founders of 21st century freedom, as will those with a superb education who turn it to the cause of freedom—rather than simple corporate profits or government power.

It is today's parents, teachers, mentors and students who will determine whether America's future is free or aristocratic. Whatever your line of work, become a leadership mentor in your field. Prepare yourself, whatever your life path, by getting a true leadership education. The future of freedom depends on regular people getting a great leadership education. If they do, freedom has a fighting chance in the 21st century. If not, the future is doomed to aristocracy. And it is already well on its way.

CHAPTER 3

The End of the Republic

*America is not so much in economic
crisis as it is in freedom crisis.*

When a national crisis occurs, those currently in power
make or break the future. Polls and blogs are quoted, but
they have no real might, and elections are long past or not yet
close enough to determine events. Actually, this is how the
Founders wanted it—so media or mob emotions wouldn't
make bad decisions when the stakes are the highest.

This system has worked well for America in the past, and it is
still the best model for the future. With that said, something
is different this time—and the difference is very dangerous.

American leaders during crisis periods have always used
Short-term Pragmatism as a basis for high-stakes leader-
ship. Washington used this method during the Revolution,
Jefferson with the Barbary Coast Pirates, Lincoln in the Civil

War, and others such as Teddy Roosevelt, FDR, Truman and Reagan made it almost synonymous with American presidential leadership. Short-term Pragmatism means doing what it takes to fix the problem, *now*, in the way most likely to end the crisis and return to normalcy. Some of the greatest failures of American history came when Presidents failed to adopt this approach—from Madison in 1812 to Carter in 1979.

When a crisis ended and normalcy returned, the method has historically shifted from Short-term Pragmatism back to what could be called Principled Realism. In theory, principles are the realm of idealism, which is the opposite of practical realism. In practice however, great Presidents and Congresses have occurred when they blended idealism and realism, practicality with principle.

In short, America has an excellent track record in crisis precisely because the Short-term Pragmatism of crisis periods occurred in an overall environment of Principled Realism.

All this changed during the first Bush administration from 1988 to 1992. Because of the change, we no longer fix crises and return to normalcy, which was the pattern of American history from 1776 to 1987. Like ancient ruins built one upon another, each crisis is layered upon the ruins of the last, sublimating new challenges on past problems. The Gulf War, the culture of scandal, the Balkans, African conflicts, hanging chads, 9/11, Afghanistan, Iraq, the energy crisis, missing WMD's, economic crises—they all build on each other and interconnect in the America psyche and soul in a strident crescendo.

By the end of the Vietnam War and Watergate, Principled Realism was under attack, and by the middle of Bush I's presidency it was practically dead. Causes of this include upgraded technology, media, and the Internet. But the nail in the coffin came in 1994 with the "Contract with America."

In this historic program, politicians took the campaign into their entire term. Today, the parties are as active between campaigning as during them, so the mud-slinging, name-calling, scandal-searching, and *ad hominem* attacks never stop. Those in power spend as much or more time defending themselves and their policies as they do anything else. And the media follow the same pattern—treating daily news like a campaign rather than a time of normalcy.

And so, what replaced Principled Realism? The answer is profound and disturbing. Perhaps the best title for the new method of American leadership comes from a recently coined phrase, "The Permanent Campaign." This is the idea that modern national leaders never really stop running for office, that they are always campaigning. Instead of winning the campaign and then settling down to governing with Principled Realism, modern leaders can never stop campaigning. *This is democratic aristocracy, not a federal republic.*

In all of this the workaday is Short-term Pragmatism—rules and wise decision-making for long-term needs is rare to non-existent. Aristocrats still apply long-term thinking to their own education, career and investment, but seldom to governing. All governance is putting out fires, or creating them for opponents. Parties run full-time, not just during the elections, and our elected officials are constantly on trial—day in and day out. Reflection, wisdom, principles, ideals, even practicality—there is no time for any of these. Short-term Pragmatism (constant, hard-nosed, often manipulative) is the name of the game in crisis and normalcy. Indeed, in this environment, crisis is normalcy.

Welcome to 21st-century politics, where statesmanship and governance are quaint historical concepts and politics is all there is.

Then a crisis comes along. Not a made-to-order crisis, which is the normal daily fare, but a real, challenging, even over-whelming crisis like 9/11, the energy crisis or the economic crisis. In past times, Short-term Pragmatism would solve immediate problems and then Principled Realism would be applied to create long-term solutions. That kept America free and prosperous for over two centuries.

But today we follow a different model. 9/11 led to a huge reduction of our freedoms and drastically increased govern-ment spending and regulation. Energy crises influenced foreign policy to the point of unprecedented American imperialism and global interventionism. The solution to the economic crisis was the government purchasing thousands of mortgages—in effect, a hostile (if invited) takeover of an

entire industry. We are witnessing the end of the Republic—
literally.

Everybody wants to be rescued, and few have any faith in
long-term Principled Realism, so all that is left is to hope the
fixes will work. Indeed, the Republic is defunct. Fortunately
(and yes, I am being sarcastic), the Empire has the power to
save us.

The aristocrats (we call them "experts" or "officials") must
save all the poor, confused peasants. Whatever crisis arises,
we turn to Washington. This is hardly what its namesake,
George Washington, had in mind.

Which provokes an interesting question: What *did* he have in
mind? In times of challenge, calm reflection upon principles
is vital. If our generation could but ask this one question:
What did Washington and his colleagues have in mind, and
how does it help us today? The more severe the crisis, the
more we need a return to principles. Short-term Pragmatism
will hopefully fix current crises, but unless a new generation of Principled Realists arises, the crises will continue to
mount.

CHAPTER 4

The Era of Liberals
and Conservatives is Over

The American Dream is not a government program.

When everything depends on which side is right, what happens when both sides are wrong?

Liberalism believes in the State: Government is the savior of mankind to guard against greedy businessmen. Conservatism today believes in the Market: Business prosperity is the solution to mankind's struggles, and the State must be controlled by business.

Both are wrong; and yet the battle continues. To judge from media and academia, the thinkers are stuck in this paradigm; to judge from elections—so, indeed, are the voters.

These are our choices (we are told), one or the other: the State or the Market. As Pat Choate has argued, the three megatrends today are the following:

- Modern Mercantilism

- Corporatism and Elitism

- National Security

Sovereignty and prosperity have been sacrificed for global market-ism and statism. It is no longer State versus Market on the national level, but a global battle where the two choices—Government or the Corporation—are part of the same team: the global aristocracy.

Ironically, as Thomas Frank shows in *The Wrecking Crew*, conservatives have used the State to promote their creed of worldwide capitalism. Likewise, liberals have emphasized the use of markets and the spread of western business to promote democratization and more "equitable" wealth distribution. America needs to lead, as Thomas Freidman argues, and he says its best bet is to lead in the world's biggest problem—that it is "hot, flat and crowded." America should lead the world to "Green," using both markets and governments—Freidman's suggestion. As Friedman says, "Green is not just a new form of generating electric power. It is a new form of generating national power—period."

Freidman is right about one thing: Neither State nor Market *alone* can win anymore. Great nations are built on great ideas, and governments and markets play their important roles in furthuring those ideas. But neither the State nor the

Corporation is a great idea *in itself*. Freedom, America's traditional Great Idea, cannot work unless both free government and free enterprise exist. The Soviet Union failed, at least in part, because its idea of equality was (perhaps) politically viable but flew in the face of market principles. The British Empire dwindled when it allowed market growth without political independence. There are many other examples.

But today, liberals still want the State to win—that is, to take over the Market and control it; while conservatives want the corporate aristocracy and global elite to control governments. Or, in other words (maybe too strong of words) the whole system is doomed.

Maybe it's good that the two sides—Government and Market—compete with each other. But a new aristocracy is running both sides of the debate, and sending the bill to taxpayers around the world. The media collaborates (after all, it is a business) as does academia (mostly a branch of government now).

So here's where we are. As Barbara Ehrenreich's book *This Land is their Land* argues, "While members of the moneyed elite can buy Congressmen, many in the working class can barely buy lunch." Her satire concludes with the suggestion to find a website that will match you perfectly with a new country to flee to in order to find freedom.

One thing is certain: As long as the aristocrats are in charge, government will grow. When liberals run it, it will grow to redistribute wealth to the global "have-nots," straight from the pockets of the middle class. When conservatives win elections, government will grow to promote global business empires and enforce taxpayer care of social needs—freeing up elite capital for more profitable uses. If this seems too cynical, consider why government doesn't shrink when both liberals and conservatives promise to reduce it. It was Bill Clinton who said that "The era of big government is over."

Today, the era of conservatives and liberals is over. Both have either become aristocrats, or their employees or agents. Ours is the era of a new, global aristocracy, which uses both governments *and* markets to increase its power and wealth. Against that stands the idea of freedom. It is an idea from the past, but its time is not over.

Freedom spreads from the people, seldom from the experts or teams of experts in whom governmental power tends to reside. This has always been true in history and it is today. We will choose in our lifetime between an era of aristocracy and an era of freedom. And it will be the "regular" people who choose. Even those who feel powerless and without resources are making the choice.

The choice is simple, if not easy. It is as simple as fearing the news versus turning it off and studying the great thinkers. It is as simple as being dependent on a job versus thinking and acting like an entrepreneur. The hallmark of aristocratic society is a mass of people who consider themselves limited, stuck, inferior.

The hallmark of freedom, in contrast, is the individual who puts aside labels or limits and lives his/her dreams. The American Dream is not a government program—it is a state of mind, a choice to be better and work harder and be independent.

If it can be said that America is in an economic crisis, it is even more so in a freedom crisis. Will our generation turn to government to solve our crises, or to ourselves to apply initiative, ingenuity, tenacity and risk to building a better world?

CHAPTER 5

Aristocratic Elections

It is the nature of power to centralize, then expand.

If one word could describe American politics, the word might well be "ironic." Why? Because people don't vote for what they want; they vote for some thing else. For most people, politics is about making compromises—voting for "the lesser of two evils." Sometimes it means voting for a candidate who sounds right on, only to watch his/her term of office develop into something else. Few people get to elect what they consider to be an ideal candidate and then feel well pleased with their official's performance. That's *ironic*.

George Lakoff's book *The Political Mind* helps us understand the irony, and why it will likely increase in the years ahead. He writes:

> "*Social change is material (who controls what wealth),*
> *institutional (who runs what powerful institutions), and*

*political (who wins elections). But the main battlefield is
the brain, especially how the brain functions below the
level of consciousness."*

Many assume that the irony of American politics is rooted in
the governmental system, or in the party system that developed after the Constitution was in place and has evolved and
increased its power ever since. Lakoff argues a deeper cause:
the brain itself. Specifically, it boils down to how the brain
understands the concept of freedom. Two groups—progressives and radicals—understand freedom quite differently:

> *"Progressives have accepted an old view of reason,
> dating back to the Enlightenment, namely, that reason
> is conscious, literal, logical, universal, unemotional,
> disembodied, and serves self-interest…this theory of
> human reason* **has been shown to be false in every
> particular, but it persists.**" [emphasis added]

This gives an "enormous advantage" to the radicals, who
couch the world as a huge culture war and are currently
promoting, quite effectively, a capitalist-controlled new
aristocracy that runs society, a government based on intimidation and obedience to this new order, manipulation of
ideas through the media, and manipulation of morals for the
masses (but not the aristos), politics, and the market.

Perhaps most importantly, the way this agenda is promoted is
drastically changing American society. It spreads its message
subtly (targeting the unconscious mind), seemingly chaotical-

ly, emotionally, heroically and iconically (through celebrity), individually and (perhaps most dangerously), popularly.

In short, both the political *views* of conservatism and liberalism are now split into two new camps: those who value wise elections, public debate, and due process versus those who value wealth, celebrity, experts, populism and emotional swaying of the masses.

Most people still use the terms "conservative" and "liberal," but if Lakoff is right, they no longer mean much. More to the point, they mean you may well be voting *against your own interests*. What choice do you have?

Lakoff believes that understanding how our minds work will help. He may have a point. After all, America was founded on the idea that we didn't need a class system, and that a class system certainly shouldn't govern us. It was founded on the ideal that we are capable of reason and wisdom and of governing ourselves in a well-structured, constitutionally-guaranteed Republic. God, nature and reason had created us equal, and "We the People" could elect leaders, oversee them through periodic elections, and maintain free government through a good constitution, checks and balances, and a wise electorate. All of this worked as long as we had two major views with shared methodology.

The Federalists and Anti-Federalists disagreed greatly on the issues, but shared the view of electing and ratifying, and following the voice of the electorate. Same with the Democratic

Republicans and the Whigs. The Civil War occurred because the two sides, Democrats and Republicans, disagreed on method: The North considered federal law higher than state; the South exactly the opposite. Since neither side would give in, violence became the solution. After the war, Democrats and Republicans again disagreed on many principles for over a century, but always engaged the conflict in the agreed-upon forums of elections and the rule of law.

In the 1960's a new methodology, or actually an old methodology vying for new ascendancy, began increasing its influence—the radical methodology of *populism*. The conservative expression of the new populism joined with the values of aristocracy, while the liberal expression emphasized global brotherhood. These interacted, conflicted, interconnected and grew through the seventies, eighties, and nineties. By the pivotal date of September 11, 2001, the world was on the verge of a major shift.

The old model was conservative versus liberal viewpoints competing in a structure of constitutional institutions and guidelines. The new model is something very different. In embryo, it includes two major ideologies: aristocracy and freedom.

Aristocracy is prevailing, because the aristo's view of the brain is more *useful* than the view adopted by most of those supporting freedom. Freedom lovers—whether they are conservative, liberal, libertarian, moralistic, green, whatever—tend to believe that people are naturally rational and literal, and that they think independently and wisely.

The Aristocratic view of the brain is very different: that the masses are easily swayed by symbol, emotion, language, models, and expert opinion. Just create the sense that "everybody" thinks a certain way and that it's popular to think that way (and Neanderthal to think otherwise), and you'll sway opinion.

The aristo method uses the same language over and over, but from different sources—media, entertainment, news, experts, academia, art, policy reports, officials, contemporary literature. "Repetition makes truth" is their motto, or "Perception is reality."

And yet, like a crazy ex-girlfriend, if their methods ever become too clear, too exposed, they respond (completely convinced of their own innocence and sincerity), "You're just imagining things! You see conspiracy *everywhere!*", or at least, "It's just business, nothing personal." We've heard this enough that it is an acceptable answer for many people. As is, "Well, he's the expert, not you." This is aristocracy at its smug and clinically-unmalicious worst.

Of course, many Americans don't like the term "aristocracy." But it is human nature to look up to celebrities, experts, and officials. Virtually every public school and most others socialize almost explicitly in order to teach these lessons so well that almost nobody ever forgets them. As Dewey noted, it is the unconscious curriculum that really does the teaching.

On a personal level, here is what this means: Probably not

everything you think about politics or the world is the result of your independent thinking. If Lakoff is to believed, much of it was influenced by aristocratic-promoted ideas and beliefs, even if you are a highly independent thinker.

If you read Lakoff, you'll learn much about being a leader—and how both good and bad leaders use things like the fundamental attribution error, reactive devaluation, the salient exemplar effect, embodied bias, linguistic bindings, and so many more. If you don't know what these mean and you care about freedom, you might do well to learn them.

The aristocratic party that is subtly, symbolically and surely conquering the globe knows these things well, and uses them. For example (one small example of thousands), you can tell when aristocrats took over conservatism by researching when conservative leaders stopped using the phrase "free enterprise" and replaced it with "free market."

Tocqueville said all great nations are run by interplay between two great parties: the aristocracy party and the "freedom" party (he said "democratic," and defined it as freedom). The aristocratic party wins by hiring those who promote its agenda. Freedom wins when good, concerned people understand what the aristos are doing well enough to thwart it by choosing an independent course rooted in the tenets of freedom.

And, as the American founders showed, the freedom party wins by cooperating with freedom-lovers from other viewpoints. In our day, those who desire freedom over aristocracy should stop fighting with other freedom lovers who differ politically and band with anyone—whatever their views— who really belongs to the freedom party. There are Aristo- crats and The Rest of Us, and freedoms wins only when The Rest of Us know what is going on and work together.

CHAPTER 6

A New Political Party?

America's biggest problem is that it has lost its purpose.

Previously, I mentioned Tocqueville's thought that great nations always struggle between the interests of the "Aristocracy Party" and the "Democratic Party." In reality the parties use different names, of course, but the simplistic labels I have chosen well represent the two forces vying for power in many nations.

The popular meaning of the word "democracy" has changed a lot since the 1830's. To really understand this, we need to realize that there are at least three major views in our day competing for societal leadership.

This chapter could be titled *Democracy versus Capitalism.* During the Cold War, words like democracy, freedom and capitalism were often used interchangeably. Any purist of political thought would cringe at these careless semantics, but many authors really did not distinguish between these three terms.

Perhaps this was natural in war time, where capitalist, democratic and freedom-focused nations were allied against communist, authoritarian and totalitarian regimes. But this all changed with the fall of the Berlin Wall, though it didn't become widely apparent just how drastic the changes would be until after 9/11. In short, the philosophy of "the enemy of my enemy is my friend" was no longer an operational imperative once the Cold War ended.

Capitalists found that their interests were often not the same as "freedom" and seldom "democratic." Democracy began to distinguish its aims from those of capitalism and freedom, and those envisioning a future of spreading freedom began to see pitfalls and roadblocks—and growing alienation from its nominal allies. And although our complacent populace still does not consciously discern the distinctions, those who actively seek to further the respective objectives sense a rift they are perhaps only starting to put a finger on.

Going back to more precise definitions, the world today is divided into at least three competing political visions. The worldviews that seek to spread these visions could quite accurately be called the Aristocracy Party, the Democracy Party and the Freedom Party.

The Aristocracy Party

The Aristocracy Party sees the world as:

- International

- Capitalistic

- Corporate

- Technological

- Pragmatic

- Competitive

- Elitist

The fundamental organizing factor of the world is economic, a division between the "haves" and the "have-nots," and a natural class system. Morals include:

- Strength

- Success

- Longevity

- Power

- *Noblesse Oblige*

Aristocrats are loyal to self, family and class, and usually consider patriotism, religion and localism quaint and middle-class.

They operate on the view that the masses are easily swayed and that the strong rule the world—and should. In this view, government is a tool of big wealth and laws apply differently to diverse classes. For example, investment law in the United States that allows people with a certain net worth to make investments their poorer family and neighbors cannot is clearly a capitalistic, aristocratic model. In international affairs, aristocrats are unilateral and use policy for profit.

The Democracy Party

The Democracy Party sees a world that is:

- Global

- Democratic

- Governmental

- Humane

- Charitable

- Cooperative

- Egalitarian

Democracy Partyists are loyal to the nation and the citizenry. Of course charity and cooperation are facilitated (read: enforced) by the government; the government is the organizing institution of society. Morals center on tolerance, providing for human needs through government programs, helping the "little guy" get ahead, and redistributing wealth to those who need it most.

Historically, religion was a central part of this view, but today church is often replaced by a cause: green, gender, etc. The Democracy group often views Aristocrats as greedy and uncaring, but shares the elitist view that the masses must be taken care of (albeit by government rather than the market). The Democracy Party considers business and private wealth to be an asset of the state and feels that the law must be used to reduce class division. When this party uses the term "democracy" it usually means "parliamentary government."

The Freedom Party

The Freedom Party (which includes many who register Republican, Democrat, Independent, other parties, and un-affiliated) is a combination of those who believe more in private solutions, whether they be anti-government libertarians, religious moralists, former liberals and conservatives, those who love the environment, minority rights, the Constitution, strong military without imperial goals, and the list goes on. The Freedom Party is:

- Localist

- Free-enterprising

- Entrepreneurial

- Familial

- Individualistic

- Creative

- Connective

Adherents believe the world is organized around individuals and families who should freely participate in whatever associations they choose—including community, commercial, social, religious, intellectual, etc.

For them, morals include the following:

- Initiative

- Tenacity

- Independence

- Friendship

- Civility

- Courage

- Enterprise

They are loyal to principles and people, and often take on what they consider to be the "establishment" (both aristos and democrats). They seldom accomplish much in practical politics, because the individuals get too focused on differences rather than building on commonalities. For example, religious, family-value party members and individualistic, environmentally-concerned libertarians seldom agree to work together—even though they have much more in common with each other than with the democratic or aristocratic crowds.

It is tempting to just call the Republicans the "Aristocrats" and the Democrats the "Democracy Party," but this is highly inaccurate. In truth, the Democratic Party includes all three groups—Democracy, Aristocrat and Freedom. So does the Republican Party. In fact, the freedom group is probably just as large as the other two. Those who really believe the Aristocratic worldview are relatively few, but they make up much of the top leadership of both major parties and a number of societal institutions.

The last few administrations have promoted the Aristocratic agenda with a few Democracy concepts thrown in—whether Bush, Clinton, Bush or Obama. If it were not such an historically prevalent pattern it would almost seem counterintuitive that the view with the fewest supporters is the most powerful! Maybe that's not so surprising, given that the form of society it promotes is aristocracy.

The real shock is that the Freedom Party almost never wins anything, despite its wide support across the nation. As I mentioned, this is because of one vital difference between the parties: *how* they do things—their *modus operandi*. Aristocrats hire experts to promote their agenda, and the Democracy crowd uses debate and diplomacy. As for the Freedom Party, there is no predominant organization or methodology, except maybe disagreement with each other and everyone else.

I wonder what would happen if the Freedom Party ever decided to engage in diplomacy and articulate its case. The last time this happened was between 1776 and 1789. Maybe it's time for a new Freedom Party in the 21st Century.

CHAPTER 7

The Economic Crisis

The more severe the crisis, the more we need a return to principles.

The political principles of Establishment and Governance are different. Unfortunately, they are little understood and seldom differentiated. In our day, this has become a serious problem—indeed, it has been for some time.

Establishment

The basic principle of establishing good government or law (also called founding, or constituting), is three-fold:

- Conglomerate

- Distinguish

- Close

Founders *conglomerate* a new agreement, constitution or

covenant by considering the far extremes and utilizing the best of both (while rejecting the worst and much of the rest of both). The two extremes represent the Elite and the Masses—anything else is not a true Conglomeration.

Athens conglomerated the needs of the aristocracy for economic freedom and the needs of the peasantry for protection from aristos into the rule of laws. Ancient Israel conglomerated theocentric dominance and slavery into a religious judiciary separated from a secular monarchy. Rome conglomerated the city's desire for power and the colonial need for self-governance into federalism; it had earlier combined lower- and upper-class differences into a republic.

Later, Europe would conglomerate Catholic and Protestant conflicts into secular legal codes with the weight of "divine" mandate. Alternatively, the Americans conglomerated the distrust of kings (1777) and the frustration with parliaments (1786) into separate branches, checked and balanced. Polybius, Cicero, Montesquieu and others had suggested it, but the Americans established it. They simultaneously conglomerated desire to win wars with the popularity of individualism and independence to establish a federal/national system. Many other examples in history exist. The formula is this:

Extreme "A"

versus

Extreme "B"

becomes

Proposal "C."

It is dialectical statecraft.

Once a Conglomerate view is established, supporters of the new model *distinguish* it. The trick is to show supporters of A how much C borrows from A and rejects B, and *vice versa* for those who supported B. And, finally, the deal is *closed* by all C supporters arguing that C is the only way—pick C or else... The worse the list of conceivable negative results, the stronger the Close.

Note that this system has been used for good and ill—for the Roman Republic *and* the Empire, the Magna Charta's great increase of freedom for the aristocrats *and* decrease of the peasantry's power, the *Federalist Papers* and the *Communist Manifesto*. Tyrannical foundings dispense with the whole equation and simply enforce the Close of the tyrant's choice. When Founders seek to meet the needs of both Elite and the Masses, Conglomeration, Distinguishing and Closing very often (not always) establish new molds based on the best of the past, applying the lessons of history while avoiding the repeat of past blunders.

At the 1787 Constitutional Convention, for example, there were three major views:

1. Abolish state governments and establish one monarchial government to rule the continent.

2. Remain separate states with few (or only treaty) agreements as a central government.

3. Create a federal equality with strong, independent states and a strong central government with independent executive, legislative, and judicial powers.

The conglomerate view won partly *because* it was a Conglomerate view—it naturally took supporters from the other views and systematically adopted any good proposal made by any of the three views or any other view. This is the advantage of Establishment by constitution over Establishment by tyrannical decree.

Governance

The basic principle of Governance is quite different. It starts and ends in different places and with different assumptions and goals. Where Establishment starts with the greatest needs of the masses and of the elite, Governance starts with two questions: What is the problem? Who are the power players?

Governance then tries to Conglomerate, Negotiate and Legislate—but it is conglomerating the views of those in power, not the needs of the people. Also, Negotiation is very different than Distinguishing. In Negotiation, the power players trade, bargain, exchange, etc., instead of simply seeking for all good and rejecting all bad. Anyone who has worked at or spent much time in a state legislature or U. S. Congress will likely tell you that simply Distinguishing and Closing are too idealistic for real life—things are Negotiated and Legislated.

But here is what that means: Congress is structurally poor at Establishing New Models.

That brings us to today. The first question in any new plan, economic or otherwise, should be whether this is an issue for Establishment or Governance. Prior to 1913, this was a simple matter of state governments or the House of Representatives initiating Governance and the Senate initiating Establishment. After the 17th Amendment passed in 1913, both houses started doing both—the individual Congressman had to decide if the major goal was to fill the needs of masses and elites (Establish) or negotiate the differences of power players (Govern). This became especially complicated with The New Deal, and even more so with growing support for internationalism from 1945 to 1989.

With the fall of the Berlin Wall, the Establishment mentality began to fade entirely from American politics. Elected officials give lip service to the needs of the people, but nearly all decisions are a conglomeration of needs and wants of power players in negotiation. Back in the day, when some Republicans and some Democrats were Establishers and others were Governors, we had a party system. Now, when almost all elected officials are engaged in Governance (many don't even know the difference), we have a power system. An aristocracy.

Which means one thing: The masses are scared, angry or

ambivalent and just want the government to "fix it," so the elite will get the government *they* want. The era of government "by the people, of the people and for the people" is over.

"We're All Socialists Now" one British newspaper headlined, as conservatives and liberals in London, Washington, and across Europe lined up in public support of government bailouts. As stock markets plummeted, the agents of elites bought up billions of dollars of assets and promoted "crisis" media reports and government bailouts which tax the middle class. It's a huge transfer of money and power from the masses to the elites. Pensions, savings, house values, stock are gone—all purchased by the aristocrats. The biggest days of market decline were huge buying days for the elite.

Remember, aristocracy is where elites tell the government what to do and government taxes the middle classes to pay for it. We should never forget that the American Revolution wasn't against the monarchy until 1776; up until then it was against the aristocracy that controlled the government. The American Founders only turned against the king when he sided with the aristocracy.

Today a new aristocracy is taking over. It is buying up the good assets and telling the government to tax the rest of us to pay for the bad assets. The masses, scared to the bone, supported this. That's the result of forty years of conveyor-belt schooling and the consistent increase of regulation in every sector of society. So far all the "fixes," "answers" and "proposals" are

Governance-minded, built on the needs of power brokers and the losses and weaknesses of Negotiation.

But there is a solution. A real solution, one that works, will start with the following:

• A clear outline of the needs of the masses.

• A clear overview of the needs of the elite.

• A Conglomeration of the best ways to get both.

And this isn't just a government issue. As Thomas Friedman wrote in *The New York Times*, "Banks and insurance companies will have to be reconstituted, merged or left to die..." [*New York Times Op Ed, 10/11/08*]. Now begins the era of Establishing, Founding, Constituting—in short, *leading* instead of managing or governing—in business, government, family, etc. Government must, as Friedman put it, "regulate the excesses without smothering the underlying innovative, entrepreneurial and risk-taking attributes of our economy, which are what will ultimately bail us out—as they always have."

What government is he talking about? Surely not Washington. But maybe he's right. Maybe, just maybe, if people can look past their fear or even just realize that regulation-minded Washington and management-minded Wall Street can never fix crises with current Governance thinking, maybe regular Americans can do what Americans have always done—go out and *make* the American dream. If we wait for government to hand it to us, or Wall Street or Hollywood or Democrats or Republicans, we'll be waiting a long time. It is time for a new generation of Americans, and others, to Establish, Found and Lead.

CHAPTER 8

Aristotechnology

Freedom is an idea from the past, but its time is not over.

Anyone interested in the future of freedom should read Jonathan Zittrain's book, *The Future of the Internet: And How to Stop It*. The picture on the hardcover edition alone is worth the price of the book. But it goes much deeper on the first page and keeps going. This is a challenging read, and the ideas covered are vital to our future.

The Internet is at a crossroads, Zittrain argues, and will go either in the direction of grassroots generativity or tethered cybersecurity. The first will increase freedom, while the second will maintain security at the cost of many aristocratic controls. Neither path is perfect, and both have some merit. Few people know how crucial this choice is or that it is being made now. Yet the future of freedom hangs on it.

This is not hyperbole. It is real, and it is timely.

The Internet has been a great source of innovation, creativity and freedom, because it has been *generative*. This means that anybody with a computer and Internet access could put whatever they wanted online. On the one hand this is a powerful freedom, but on the other hand there have been many abuses.

Online, person A's opinion has the same weight as person B's. But what if person A is a seventeen-year-old Nazi sympathizer? The proponents of generativity argue that over time most people will listen to reason and we can trust that the outcome will work out well. Others wonder—what about the six or eighteen who do listen to the Nazi promoter? School shootings and terrorist bombings give credence to the idea that some type of regulation may be warranted.

If anybody can say anything online, what of accuracy, decency, or safety? Internet promoters make a lot of money passing around false messages, without the editors that perform a measure of check on the print and broadcast media. Is it the destiny of the Internet to be the major provider of yellow journalism, child pornography, and shadiness? Strong words, but the reality is even stronger. Is the generative future viable without a balance of freedom and order?

The other future is the "tethered appliance," as Zittrain calls it. Instead of a two-way communication, this type of technology allows the user to call, email or otherwise use the iPhone, TiVo, OnStar, the Internet, software or other technology. Sometimes a central operator controls the flow and edits it to ensure safety and perhaps even accuracy or decency. For example, if a user downloads copyrighted material illegally and then sends it to a friend, the technology *provider* is liable and will likely not allow the transfer. In tethered appliances, the provider can monitor the usage. For example, TiVo was able to report that Janet Jackson's performance was rewound three times more often than any other part of Super Bowl XXXVIII.

But of course, if the provider can monitor users, government can too. What does this mean for the future of privacy?

Zittrain is a supporter of generativity, and very concerned about the loss of freedom that a tethered society would bring. But the challenge to freedom goes much deeper. In fact, even the generative technologies are easily tethered. With spyware your personal computer work can be monitored—by private or government watchers. Your conversations while driving can be listened to if you have OnStar, and, of course, phone calls can be overheard.

As digital technology increases, perhaps anything and everything can be watched—by companies, individuals and governments.

Personal papers, documents, conversations—nothing is private in a digital world. The solution has little to do with generativity versus tethering, and more to do with separations, checks and balances. Technology gives governments more power, and so the need for Constitutional overrides is even stronger. I've heard it said that the U.S. Constitution was made for an agrarian people, and is therefore inadequate for our day. In actual fact, our modern technologies make the Constitutional checks and balances more important now than ever. If anything, we may need even stronger ones!

Amazingly, the 1789 U.S. Constitution solves the current "generativity versus tethering" question. It allows both, and keeps both within proper boundaries. Some regulation is needed, or we'll be stuck with privacy for aristocrats (who can afford it) and aristocratic surveillance of everyone else in practically all aspects of life. Under a fully operational constitutional model, *privacy would be regulated and maintained by the right people in the right way—with oversight by the people*, and effective checks and balances. Under our current model, this is disappearing.

Since 1945 there has been a gradual, some would say rapid, de-emphasis of the clear separations, checks and balances of the Constitution. In practice, this is a tragedy. Today, more than ever, we need a citizenry who demands that the Constitution be followed—as it is on paper, not as "experts" have interpreted it. And that's not a criticism of the judiciary or executive alone. If anything, it is Congress and the state legislatures which are most to blame. Fortunately, they are the closest to the people, and therefore the most likely to change. But change will only come when people—"regular" people—read, study, understand and support the U.S. Constitution.

In general, technology is a great benefit to prosperity, security, lifestyle and progress. Adopting effective principles of freedom actually allows technology to progress more quickly without tethering its users to an aristocratic Big Brother. When technology flourishes, power increases. But power can be used for or against freedom. Progress is measured by the increase or decrease of freedom *and* technology. When both are prevalent, society progresses and prospers. When both are diminished, society regresses. But the real value of this measurement tool is the gap between the two.

When technology is high and freedom low, power centralizes in the aristocratic or autocratic few and society, happiness and prosperity decline. While some few do find success, society as a whole degenerates.

When freedom is high and technology low, freedom itself naturally foments technological progress. Sometimes a nation in this situation is conquered by a stronger power before it completes its technological growth, but high freedom tends to catalyze technological growth.

In contrast, low freedom always blocks or at the very least slows technology.

History provides this clear lesson for our day: Tethered technology is a means of rule, not leadership, and eventually decreases or drastically slows technological progress.

Some would argue that this model is flawed, that it leaves out morality (be it fidelity in marriage or responsible protection of the environment). But morality is technology in the best sense—strong family and environmental values and practices meet all the criteria of the best technologies and increase progress, power, prosperity and freedom when applied by a society.

Freedom is neither anti-technology nor pro-technology *patently*. Freedom principles are against tethered, controlling, manipulative and aristocratic technologies or uses, and strongly support technological progress and freedom together.

CHAPTER 9

A New American Strategy

America must stand for something besides power—
it must deserve to lead.

In Phillip Bobbitt's book, *Terror and Consent: The Wars for the Twenty-first Century*, he argues that we are in a new world reality. Where the major American challenge of the twentieth century was to defeat our enemies (fascism, communism, totalitarianism) without taking on their characteristics, the fundamental problem now is to confront the challenges of terror while simultaneously maintaining "official accountability in the face of largely hypothetical threats that require anticipatory action based on secret intelligence."

In other words, we must structure governmental forms and policies that effectively gather, analyze and act on secret information, and find ways to keep those who know the secrets from using them in a way that reduces freedom.

Needless to say, this is a huge challenge.

The American framers created, through the U.S. Constitution, a system where power was separated, checked, and balanced. The state powers were separated, checked and balanced by federal powers and the federal by state powers. Executive, legislative and judicial powers were separated at both levels and they, in turn, checked and balanced each other.

Hopefully, any high school student can explain this. What is often forgotten, however, is that these types of checks were "auxiliary," as *The Federalist Papers* put it. Not auxiliary as in unnecessary, but auxiliary as in *secondary*, vital backups. The primary check was the ongoing vigilance of the people. The name for such a system is freedom.

This worked incredibly well from at least 1789 to 1955, empowering government to fulfill its role in protecting the nation while at the same time keeping government from infringing on the freedoms of its citizens—like nearly all governments of history. Then in 1955 the Soviet Union began building its atomic arsenal, and the Cold War turned governments more toward secrecy. If that secrecy now has to monitor the whole globe, seeking out threats and responding before a terrorist strike, how can we possibly stop a massive reduction of privacy and freedom?

Bobbitt goes on to discuss the danger that in responding to the terrorist threat we are in danger of adopting the belief that the ends justify the means. He discusses both sides of this idea, and suggests that we are fighting for the rule of law and better be sure that this fight doesn't compromise our ability to defend ourselves.

This is bigger than most people realize, and the easy answers aren't good enough. On one extreme, the idea is that whatever it takes to maintain our defense is good—even if that means reduced freedom and a secret government. At the other extreme, the argument is that we should get rid of any and all secrecy and just let the government decide under the original constitutional rules—even though terrorists will strike before we can respond. There are many mid-road arguments, such as declaring war officially on terrorism and responding to it through military channels.

The complexity of this issue demands that this discussion be widespread. I hope you'll read Bobbitt's book and really think about it. And I hope you'll re-read the Constitution and The Federalist Papers and really think about them. Then I hope you'll go a step further and engage the dialog.

Terrorism is an immediate threat. A secretive government is a long-term threat. What should we do? Seriously: *What would Washington do—or Jefferson?* We need leaders like them today. And the only way we'll get them is if regular citizens really think about these things, pay the price to arrive at an informed, principled opinion and share their conclusions. We need men and women of sound understanding to reason and debate, to plan and to act. More, we need to see the big picture.

Futurist John Naisbitt wrote in *Mindset* that success in the 21st Century will go to the opportunity leaders, not the problem solvers. America hasn't yet figured this out. The focus of our leaders—political, corporate, academic, media—seems mostly on problems. For example, argues Fareed Zakaria, the current debate in the United States is totally out of touch with the global reality.

The news covers Iraq, Afghanistan, Iran and North Korea, as do the weekly talk shows. Americans are "obsessed with issues like terrorism, immigration, homeland security, and economic panics." But these all represent a preoccupation with the global losers of the past twenty years. Zakaria argues that the "real challenges that the country faces come from the winners, not the losers, of the new world." (See his excellent book, *The Post-American World*.)

How much are Americans thinking of the real challenges ahead, from China, Brazil, South Africa, Kenya, India and Russia? These emerging powers are on the rise economically and politically—yet most Americans are alarmingly unaware. The economic growth of these nations is increasing their clout and "producing political confidence and national pride." The American people and the United States government are unprepared to deal with these new powers and their demands, choices and might. The central role of the United States in the world is about to drastically shrink, even as Washington sees America as the world's last superpower. American political, economic and psychological letdown is inevitable.

Many of the rising powers have sectors with free economics, less regulation, lower taxes and more opportunity than the United States. Entrepreneurs are increasingly courted and rewarded in these nations, while they are increasingly regulated and put down in the U.S. and Western Europe. The United States has a great choice ahead: Increase taxes to protect jobs and benefits, or free up the economy in order to really compete in the decades ahead. The first is socialism, the second is free enterprise. But here is the great challenge: The first is seen as "fixing the economy," and the second as scary, and probably depressionary. A scarcity mentality is the cause of socialism; abundance is the foundation of free enterprise. Clearly, America today is caught in the grip of scarcity.

And there you have our current irony. The story most Americans know is of a powerful but fearful great nation that leads the world against dark and sinister forces of jihadism and dictatorship. What is left out of the story are the two dozen nations that are growing and prospering without being affiliated with either side.

Washington will be forced to rethink its domestic and global strategy—forced not by its enemies but by its competitors. They are refusing to allow its meddling, and they are starting to attract those who are seeking free markets, opportunity and freedom. On top of all this, at the same time that Americans are losing faith in *their* government, the new powers are experiencing a surge of nationalism and they want to be seen as strong and to spread their ways and power like the U.S. has for so long. As the U.S. mires itself in the worst problems around the world, the new powers are attracting capital, technology and leadership by offering opportunity and freedom.

Of course, the U.S. can solve this all in one simple way: Become the most inviting nation on earth. Get rid of massive regulation and simply re-establish freedom, free enterprise and free markets—true *opportunity*. To do this, it will have to stop interfering in world conflicts and trying to be more socialist than Canada or India. If it fails in either change, if it doesn't deregulate and stop policing the world, it will decline and collapse in power as did Rome, Spain, France and Britain—all of whom followed the same limping path to failure. China, Russia and India will be the new superpowers.

It is troubling, from a self-interested American perspective, that hegemony is no longer a given; but America's biggest problem is that it has lost its *purpose*. It became the world's leader by promoting freedom, and it lost its purpose when its major goal became power. The freedom purpose had animated and informed its domestic and international actions, and this made it great.

Power as purpose—both at home and abroad—turned Washington into a place hated around the world, and by its own citizens. Crowds cheered in the movie *Independence Day* when the White House exploded—*American* crowds. The United States is powerful in many ways but not in one critical way: legitimacy. Much of the world sees the U.S. as powerful, yes—but *only* powerful. Not good, or great, or standing for something. The United States of America has become the world's upper class, and it governs like an aristocracy. In fact, more and more it *is* an aristocracy. Even Europe wants to backlash against growing American elitism.

For America to maintain a leadership role in the decades ahead, it must stand for something. Thomas Friedman thinks it should stand for global Green. But I'm convinced that freedom is its only path to success. Without a renewed commitment to freedom—free government, deregulation, free enterprise—America doesn't *deserve* to lead the world. America must stop policing the world and start standing for its one greatest export—freedom. Unless this happens, it won't solve its own problems or be able to help anyone else.

CHAPTER 10

Elitism vs. Wisdom

*The U.S. can solve this all in one simple way—
become the most inviting nation on earth.*

Perhaps nothing dominates our era more than the rise of a
new aristocracy—global, secular, elitist, driven, arrogant.
The new aristocracy is taking over governments and business, institutions and nations.

The top agents of the aristocrats are generally highly trained.
They are usually experts, and they often combine the ego of
expertise with an alarming dependence on other experts. They
are seldom patriotic, and look with amusement or disdain on
those who are. Their allegiance is to career success, which
they approach with the dedication and fervor of a religion.
They believe in status, personal wealth and celebrity. They see
society as a list of status levels that would overwhelm a French
courtier. They increasingly run the nation—all nations.

These, of course, are generalizations. They also happen to be generally true. This may be the next great challenge of the 21st Century, because aristocracy is inherently incompatible with freedom.

History seems a long proof of the Other Golden Rule: "He who has the gold makes the rules." Political history of the world is the story of aristocracy versus monarchy, and oligarchy versus tyranny. Freedom, the kind envisioned by Adam Smith, Montesquieu, Jefferson, Adams, Madison, Bastiat, etc., is democratic—the regular people are free.

Yet the new aristocracy uses the words "democracy" and "capitalism" almost interchangeably with "freedom." There is great confusion in this, as the masses tend to acquiesce to these definitions without examining them.

Michael Novak cites the familiar Polish joke that capitalism is the exploitation of man by man, whereas socialism is the opposite. In truth, there are at least two types of socialism and two kinds of capitalism.

Aristocratic Socialism, or Communism, occurs when one elite group wrests power from the others, then redistributes wealth between everyone not part of their group.

Democratic Socialism allows the populace to vote for the elites who rule them.

Aristocratic Capitalism creates a market-government alliance which rigs the system in favor of the wealthy, and allows the middle class to work for and even compete with elites, but with different levels of commercial rules.

Finally, Democratic Capitalism establishes and maintains a truly free enterprise system where all people are treated equally by the law, including the commercial codes.

Of these, only Democratic Capitalism is democratic—the other three systems are always run by elites. These elites often call themselves supporters of democracy (democratic socialists) or capitalism (aristocratic capitalists). These two groups predominate in Europe, Washington, and both the Democrat and Republican Parties. They are both elitist.

In comparing these two latter groups, there is one major difference—the "democrats" are more typically meritocratic while the "capitalists" tend to be more aristocratic in their elitism. For example, American Democrats decry business and glorify credentials, while Republicans alienate minorities and honor wealth. Both sides see the world as grades of people, and the object is to rise in grade.

Our biggest institutions—from public schools to elderly care centers and factories to corporate high rises—reinforce this grade system of caste/class. Parents counsel their children in patently class terms. Even the word itself, "class," is used in schools as the center of our learning experience. Whatever the curriculum, the place we learn is class; a connotation we might extrapolate is that we learn how to best stay in our class and serve the upper classes, or (at best) rise within our class.

Both major elite groups seek worldwide acceptance, loyalty, and support. Their ideas and ideals are discussed in Thomas Sowell's *The Vision of the Anointed*, *Revolt of the Elites* by Christopher Lasch, *Rise of the Meritocracy* by Michael Young, *Privilege* by Ross Douthat, and any of several books by David Brooks. For both types of elites, economic success is the ultimate goal.

But neither Democrat-style social democracy nor Republican-like aristocratic capitalism is compatible with freedom.

Unfortunately, the masses vote for and support elites from the social democratic and aristocratic capitalist camps—election after election. They watch their high hopes crumble, then make the same mistake next election. As Christopher Lasch put it, "Meritocracy is a parody of democracy."

Democratic capitalism requires three things (which the American Founders called a democratic republic, and Michael Novak elaborates on these principles in *The Spirit of Democratic Capitalism*):

1. A free government, where power is separated, checked and balanced effectively.

2. A free enterprise economy, where enterprise is encouraged and supported by law and non-governmental factors, and government treats all citizens and legal entities equally.

3. Strong morals, families, and voluntary communities

(non-governmental), which see charity and service as virtues and engage them adequately to meet the needs of the disadvantaged.

Without all three, the system is neither Democratic Capitalism nor free enterprise. Indeed, if #3 is missing, the system is classified as Aristocratic Capitalism, which emphasizes greed, exploitation, imperialism and war. It also quickly dismantles #2, and eventually #1.

If the Social Democrats gain power, they erode #1 and #2 with government programs in lieu of a voluntary #3. They say that without government such problems would never be fixed. This leads to massive regulations, drastically decreased freedom, and a welfare state with large majorities dependent on government. Entrepreneurs and capital flee, and the economy tanks.

The "problem" with free enterprise (or Democratic Capitalism), the reason it seldom lasts long, is that when all three are working, the aristocracy loses status. When this happens, elites do whatever it takes to get it back. Social democrat elites and aristocratic capital elites do different things, blame each other, and both win—the aristocracy grows no matter which side wins the election. Election after election, year after year, aristocracy gains power and momentum.

And while the masses complain, they seem only to get the big picture when they're harping over checkers; and these blips of awareness don't appear to affect their subsequent behavior in the voting booth. The masses don't see what is happening, but they still buy into the elite game: Whoever gets more mass votes wins for now and gets to increase the aristocracy; masses who don't like it should find a way to join the aristocracy. The worst-case scenario would be true freedom, a real free enterprise system of democratic capitalism with no perks of elite status. But this is aristocracy pure and simple—sometimes progressive, other times conservative, but always *aristocratic*.

Is this the America we want?

The irony is that most Americans don't want it. They want a true freedom, real economic mobility, the liberty and opportunity that free enterprise affords. They want government to do its part, and they want non-governmental groups to do their great part as well. They want it to work. They just want America to work.

America became great because of a certain type of freedom—all three pieces of democratic capitalism applied simultaneously. These three are still the success formula, for the United States and any other people brave and smart enough to establish them.

CHAPTER 11

Domesticating Aristocracy

America became great because of a certain type of freedom.

The American founding generation did something truly amazing—they tamed the aristocracy. Their work was so effective that it was still taming the aristocracy in the 1860's (the South) and 1960's (racial aristocracy). History is the long story of aristocracy controlling society, at times one faction of it ruling in monarchy but eventually the aristocracy winning out. Over and over. In our modern world, where the aristocracy is once again taking over, it behooves anyone who cares about freedom to answer this question: **How did the Founders do it?**

There may be other ways to do it, but the Founders are the only ones we know of in history to put the common people on the same level as the aristocracy. Moses came close, but upon his death the aristocracy arose almost immediately.

Saracen and Confucian greatness was highly aristocratic, as was Athenian "democracy." The list spans all of known history. Only the American Founders established a model that endured, and even expanded the freedoms of the masses after their lifetime.

One theory is that the religious people of New England loved equality. Upon examination however, this theory is clearly flawed. Religion is often even more aristocratic than economics, and the New England religion was more aristocratic than most. One principle of American Calvinism does support democratic society, however—the principle of "The Priesthood of All Believers." This doctrine allows and requires each congregation to appoint its leaders—putting ultimate power over who rules in the hands of the people.

This leads to another theory of America's success in ending rule by the upper class—the idea of giving the purse strings to the House of Representatives, elected directly by the masses. Historically, however, the aristocracy simply undid mass power by taking over any such body. Or, if this failed, the bourgeois leaders of such a body eventually started acting like an aristocracy anyway.

Another theory is that aristocratic rule was overcome by federalism—the split sovereignty of national and state governments, with the bulk of power left to the states. The flaw is that in reality the states were more controlled by aristocratic families than the federal government ever was.

All three of these—popular elections built on a moral disdain for aristocracy, mass election of the House with its power over finances, and a strong federal system—were included in the separations, checks and balances with which the Founders established freedom from class rule. But the genius came in a surprising way—surprising but obvious, elegant and precise.

Aristocracies rule according to one basic principle: They establish two sets of rules—one for themselves and another for everyone else. Even in nations of law like Britain and France, the same courts treated people differently depending on their caste. Laws favored people of a certain economic status over others.

The brilliance of the founding, as John Adams explained, is that the aristocrats were given their own club: *the Senate*. Why would the most aristocratic aspire to the House, when it was elected by the masses and only held a term of two years? Or the presidency, with its shorter four-year term and all its appointments pending approval by the Senate? No, "Senator" was the status position of the U.S. Constitution— six-year terms, oversight of everything presidential, and election by the elites of your own state. As Adams predicted, aristocratic types would seek the Senate, and therein spend most of their energy battling each other.

It is the nature of power to centralize then expand. The framers therefore controlled aristocratic power by making the Senate appealing to America's aristocrats while clearly enumerating all Senate powers and checking any expansion of these powers.

Result: A society less ruled by class than any in history.

Of course, the aristocracy fought back. But before the 17th Amendment, nearly all the fighting was done in the Senate—with little, if any, increase in the power of the aristocracy. When the 17th Amendment passed, the era of freedom began to decline—back to business-as-usual history with the aristocracy in charge.

Still, it took a whole century for aristocracy to regain control of society; the founding model was *that* brilliant. And during that century, freedom continued to increase in many arenas— even as it was being eroded at the top.

An aristocracy is only an aristocracy when it operates above the law, with its own set of rules. When the aristocracy is limited by the law, empowered in its own club and limited by that club, it is tamed. This is a "natural" aristocracy, and the masses are free, in contrast to the rule of a wealth aristocracy (capitalism), a power aristocracy (socialism), or a single aristocrat (dictatorship).

The challenge of the 21st Century is how to slow the rise of global aristocratic rule and regain freedom. The U.S. Constitutional method is the only one that has worked in history— our modern freedom lovers must find a way to establish a model based on such principles, or find something better. The future of freedom depends on it.

CHAPTER 12

Aristotrends

*Aristocracy will likely continue as long as we refuse
to face our major societal traps.*

While the biggest trend in our time, perhaps since America's Civil War in the 1860's, is the return of aristocratic dominance to the U.S., a number of other trends are drastically changing our world toward aristocracy. First, we'll discuss several traps we face that strengthen the rise of aristocracy and the demise of freedom. Then we'll consider the counter-trend that could end up helping freedom displace aristocratic rule.

A trap is neither a simple test nor a lasting trial. Tests are external challenges that we should overcome, while trials can be internal or external and must be endured. In contrast, traps are internal flaws or weaknesses that keep us from rising to meet challenges. The problems posed by traps are not external. We are the problem. Fix us, and the external challenges are more easily handled.

People seldom fix their traps until the external pain of remaining trapped grows worse than the pain of changing oneself. Nations follow this same tendency. Aristocracy will likely continue to grow as long as we refuse to face our major societal traps, including the following:

- The Treasury Trap

- The Trilateral Trap

- The Trap of the Top

- The Terrorism Trap

- The Tribo-national Trap

- The Training Trap

- The True Trap

The Treasury Trap

Economic crises are not the problem; they are just the external challenge or symptom. The root cause, or deeper problem, is that we are trapped in thinking that government is the solution to economic problems and each new crisis in the economy. In fact, freedom is the solution. Yet we are trapped, turning to the Treasury Department for solutions it is not capable of providing.

This reliance on government and dependence on force *is* the problem. It empowers the aristocracy, which uses private solutions for its own finances even as it increases its power over the masses through government controls. Of course, some government action is helpful—but only to the extent that it solves the short-term emergencies in a broader context of increasing economic freedom. Such wisdom is rare as long as we are caught in the Treasury Trap.

The Trilateral Trap

There are actually three "worlds" in our world, yet we operate as if the three are separate and unrelated. World One consists of "democratic" nations versus "enemy" nations, and such was the operating view of the twentieth century and most modern political thought.

World Two is the community of rising new economic powers that will soon become military and political powers.

World Three is the disenfranchised, the poor of the world who claim little affiliation with any nation or institution of power. Our trap is that we treat the world only on Level One, ignoring the growing, pressing realities of the other two. All three live in one, the same, *this* world. The trilateral view which separates the three is inaccurate and aristocratic. Real solutions will actually benefit all, not just those of World One.

The Trap of the Top

At a time when the United States most needs allies to promote freedom, it is losing its natural allies on many sides. When those at the top serve, they become beloved leaders. When the top dominates, controls and demands, it becomes feared and hated. Regardless of Machiavelli's views, freedom is inconsistent with this second type of ruler. In the history of nations, great powers which chose to lead by fear and power eventually found imperialism inevitable—Rome, Spain, France, Britain and Russia are examples. In contrast, the United States determined to lead other nations by example—it sought to be helpful and respected, rather than feared and obeyed. This general attitude changed in the late 1960's.

As the U.S. became a superpower, it followed the example of other failed top powers before it, seeking to be feared and obeyed. It created its own trap. Today, staying at the top is priority one, and any suggestion that inspiration is better than domination is strongly resisted—by many liberal and conservative leaders alike. This trap has led to policies and attitudes which alienate practically everyone. The gap between the U.S. and Europe widens each year on many levels. The same is true in relations with Russia, China and India. The distrust between the U.S. and Latin America is increasing, and so are conflictual attitudes between the U.S. and Japan; even relations with Canada are often tense.

As the U.S. feels its dominance slipping, it tightens its hard power apparatus—further alienating enemies, allies and neutrals. In its increasingly desperate attempt to stay at the top, it offends friend and foe alike. In all this, it turns wary eyes toward its own people as well. To put this in perspective: Would you rather live in an America that is the world's lone super power, wary of usurpation and quick to intervene globally in its great goal to remain at the top, or in an America concerned with freedom, prosperity and goodness, and genuinely happy for the rise of other nations with like goals?

The Terrorism Trap

Free governments were created to protect people from threats. In ancient times, the great threat was marauders, bandits and pirates, and states were established to thwart them—with kings, knights, castles, gated walls, etc. As these states grew, *they* became the greatest threats, so governments were built to protect citizens from the aggression of other governments. In ancient times, aristocracy arose as the natural companion of kingly governments, while in modern times free citizens proved better supports of strong governments than slaves, peasants or socialist employees. The more freedom and property citizens owned and controlled privately, the stronger the nation. Thus, the pre-modern state flourished with the aristocracy, and the modern state with truly free economics and politics.

Now we enter the post-modern age, where both threats are again present—marauders *and* states. The marauders are now called terrorists. Their threat is real, but to remodel the state to effectively thwart terrorism we are naturally reverting to our past—with aristocracy poised to dominate our future as this trend continues.

To be truly post-modern, our statesmen must establish systems which simultaneously protect us from terrorists *and* state attacks on life, liberty, property and the pursuit of happiness. The principles of freedom, best established in the U.S. Constitution, are key to this process: separate, check and balance. Empower institutions that are up to the tasks at hand—protection from terrorism and foreign powers—and effectively separate, check and balance these institutions. Give final oversight to the people. Maintain a free enterprise economy and free government with most issues decided at local levels.

In times of terrorism, nuclear warheads and other weapons of mass destruction, the application of freedom principles is more important than ever. Ancient states had rulers, modern states had leaders, and post-modern states will need statesmen. Terrorism is not a call to more secrecy and increased government power, but rather a bold reminder that freedom structures must bind down the power of any government— empowering it to act with strength while requiring it to do so with the principles and forms that maintain freedom.

Where ancient monarchy depended on the generational wisdom of aristocratic families, free government has taught us to establish and maintain Constitutions—and adhere to them. This is the real message of terrorism.

The Tribo-national Trap

The world is split in allegiance. Most of the power rests in a minority of the world's population that is steeped in a *national* culture, while the majority of the world's people are culturally *tribal*. Both national and tribal societies have natural strengths, and there are positive and negative examples of both. But the split is a huge barrier to progress in the 21st Century. Where national cultures define themselves by economics, technology and laws, tribal societies are more linked to family, community, relationships and beliefs. Both sides have much to learn from the other—indeed the biggest challenges of each are strengths of the other!

Imagine how much national culture could teach tribal society about prosperity and rule of law, and how much successful tribal cultures have to teach national societies about relationships and happiness. The trap is that neither side believes the other has much to teach it—or, where they do, it is with the inclination to abandon all in favor of the other.

National societies arrogantly see tribal cultures as backward, poor and inferior, while tribalists tend to see the national as dishonest, scheming, untrustworthy, immoral, greedy and controlling. Neither side is open to hearing the great lessons the other could teach. This strengthens aristocracy within nations, as well as globally. Some of the greatest leaders and statesmen of our time will be those who find how to bridge this chasm positively and effectively.

The Training Trap

The American Founders created the most successful nation in history by dis-establishing the aristocracy and facilitating a classless society. The long-term key to maintaining classlessness was education. Throughout history education has been the path to freedom. In class societies, the upper classes are educated, while the masses who serve them are, at best, trained.

Training consists of narrow skills and expertise in a specialization, while *education* is broad understanding of many fields, the history of humanity and, above all, the ability to think on the broad scale and see details in the context of human history, philosophy, ideas, the powerful stories of literature and media, technology, etc.

The first law the newly-created U.S. Congress passed after the Constitution was ratified was the Northwest Ordinance, which established that every territory and community would provide education to the populace (to qualify the territory for statehood).

For example, the education of Abraham Lincoln was rooted in the Bible, Shakespeare and Euclid. This was education, not training. Lincoln later sought training, but the education came first. Consider the audience that sat for hours and hours listening to the Lincoln-Douglas debates, or their progenitor farmers who read and debated *The Federalist Papers*—these people were *educated*.

With such education among the masses, the evolution of a classless free society was natural. Aristocracy cannot control such a people. Aristocracy requires that only the few are broadly educated, while the rest have narrow training and with it a natural dependency on a job.

Of course, training is a good thing. But there is a huge difference between a society with a few educated and the masses trained, and one where the masses are both educated and trained. But a highly-trained and poorly-educated population, as Allan Bloom said in *The Closing of the American Mind*, is a problem—as Nazi Germany proved.

The "True" Trap

Civilization exists where there are shared values. Indeed the word "savage" is usually applied to someone with different values. In our world today, we have a serious "truth" trap. If anyone mentions values, goodness, or says that something is "true," she can count on being asked, "Whose values?" "Whose truth?" and "Who made you the truth monitor?" Without shared values and standards of truth, there is no shared civilization. Today we have more of a competing "wild west" of factions than a shared civilization.

For example, Republicans are often criticized for their attitudes of racial aristocracy, such as their stand against Latino immigration, while Democrats are criticized for their aristocratic bias for credentialization and patronizing attitudes toward others. Even within the parties there is little agreement on which values should be shared. This is not mere disagreement on the issues or specific policies, but a deep distrust and difference of basic attitudes, core beliefs, and worldviews. Change has come to America at the beginning of the 21st Century, but there is little shared vision of what the change should look like.

Historically, aristocrats have valued the virtues of loyalty, honor, strength, lineage and wealth; the meritocratic virtues emphasized status, intelligence, tolerance and progress; warrior societies most valued fortitude, tradition, bravery and generosity; and free societies highly valued initiative, courage, resiliency, wisdom and voluntarism. Those who support freedom should be able to find much common ground in these virtues, but to date, our society seems more prone to emphasize differences, weaknesses and problems than to cooperate as a community of shared values.

Some might argue that we have the shared national value of prosperity, or economic success. "It's the economy, stupid," as the Clinton campaign put it. But what about well-funded racism or Nazism—certainly these aren't part of our shared belief in prosperity? The growing New Age movement, which has almost become mainstream now, promotes world brotherhood, peace, and love as our shared value. But what if it were enforced by "Big Brother"? Is it a shared value if government must enforce it?

Conclusion

The future of America, and the world, depends on a resurgence of understanding of and support for the shared value of freedom. By freedom I mean what Michael Novak called "the spirit of democratic capitalism" and what I prefer to call constitutional free enterprise. Again, this definition of freedom establishes government strong enough to do what it should while adequately separated, checked and balanced, and puts strong family culture, free enterprise businesses, healthy communities, free religions and media and quality schools that educate and train everyone (regardless of class), all on the same level as government. In free society, each of these naturally checks any abuses of the others.

The two places I know of that teach freedom this clearly are the classic books of history and liberal arts schools and colleges that utilize the classic books. Almost everyone else teaches aristocracy—even if they don't openly acknowledge or recognize it. Allan Bloom ended *The Closing of the American Mind* with his doubt that freedom could survive in America without the classic works as part of our widespread education of the masses. Unfortunately, it appears he was right. The future of freedom is very much in question, and if it disappears in America it may be many generations before it rises again somewhere. The future of freedom is now at stake, and unfortunately aristocracy is growing and has the upper hand.

The Mini-Factory Freedom Shift

Freedom flourishes when the people are independent,
free, and as self-sufficient as possible.

As strange as it sounds, one of Gandhi's most powerful tools used to liberate India from British rule was the spinning wheel. The British controlled most of India's industry, including textiles. Realizing that, in the words of Hamilton, "...a power over a man's subsistence amounts to a power over his will," Gandhi encouraged Indians to become more economically self-reliant by spinning their own cloth.

He wrote, "I came reluctantly to the conclusion that the British connection had made India more helpless than she ever was before, politically and economically...She has become so that she has little power of resisting famines. Before the British advent, India spun and wove in her millions of cottages just the supplement she needed for adding to her meager agriculture resources. [The British] do not know that a subtle but effective system of terrorism and organized display of force on one hand, and the deprivation of all powers of retaliation and self-defense on the other, have emasculated the people and induced in them a habit of simulation." The spinning wheel, therefore, became a symbol of economic independence, a movement that extended far beyond textile production.

After detailing the staggering depth and breadth of America's cultural, political, and economic problems, on the surface mini-factories may seem like using a BB gun to take down an elephant. Nothing could be further from the truth. Just as the spinning wheel was at the heart of Gandhi's revolution, successful mini-factories strike at the root of America's problems: apathy, dependence, bureaucracy, educational deterioration and indoctrination, national arrogance, social stratification, expediency at the expense of principle. Dependence upon corporations, federal programs, and "experts" for food, clothing, "security," benefits, health, and education has emasculated the American population.

The crippling fallacy of the activist/populist freedom movement—the reason why the freedom camp fails to gain traction—is the focus on top-down, outside-in solutions. While they have their place and can lead to positive change, marches on Washington, Tea Parties, political lobbying and activism are largely "fix-it-now" counterfeits for what can only be generational, bottom-up, inside-out solutions.

Earlier I wrote that, to regain freedom, either the aristocracy must voluntarily relinquish power and privilege, or the masses must retake their freedoms through mini-factories. The challenge is this: At no time in history have aristocratic rulers ever ceded power of their own accord. Revolution has always been needed to wrest power from the elites, and such revolution is almost always violent. An even deeper challenge is that most revolutions fail to secure lasting freedom; they generally replace one aristocracy with another.

The American Revolution was a stunning exception. And it broke the typical revolutionary mold for a reason: It was preceded by a healthy shift in the culture and perspective of the people. As John Adams wrote, "What do we mean by the American Revolution? Do we mean the American war? The Revolution was effected before the war commenced. The Revolution was in the minds and hearts of the people; a change in their religious sentiments, of their duties and obligations…This radical change in the principles, opinions, sentiments, and affections of the people was the real American Revolution."

If we are to re-establish freedom—and if it is to last generationally—then our Freedom Shift must spring from within the minds and hearts of individuals. It must be enacted by individuals, families, businesses, and communities who accept the responsibility of freedom, rather than forcing Washington to accept a list of demands. In other words, We the People must *replace* the elites, not just compel them to do what we want them to do (which will never happen).

It's often observed that pornography flourishes because people buy it. The same could be said of anything else. Government-sponsored and -protected corporations thrive because we choose to depend on them. Public schools continue operating at sub-par levels because we choose to stick with them. Investment firms rake in management fees, even as our accounts shrink, because we continue to trust them blindly. More bailouts are rolled out, crumbling businesses and industries are artificially propped up and nationalized, and the Fed printing presses press on because these measures are either welcomed by the masses, or they don't realize the long-term ramifications. We can blame the elites and spend our time and energy fighting them, or we can simply replace them by making them obsolete through organic decentralization.

The core strength of the mini-factory model is less about physical products and services, and more about the mindset, the worldview, the type of individual that mini-factories produce. In *The Other Greeks*, Victor Davis Hanson places the triumph of Western Civilization squarely on the back of ancient Greek farmers, or *geôrgoi*, arguing convincingly that farming produced a certain type of individual that inevitably led to free civilization.

"The typical Greek farmer," wrote Hanson, "...has no boss, stands firm in battle 'squarely upon his legs'...a man who judges the sophist in the assembly by the same yardstick he prunes vines and picks olives, and so cannot be fooled...

He has no belly for the prancing aristocrat and even less for the mob on the dole...And because he suffers no master, he speaks his due, fights his own battles, and leaves an imprint of self-reliance and nonconformity, a legacy of independence that is the backbone of Western society." He continues, "Their achievement was the precursor in the West of private ownership, free economic activity, constitutional government, social notions of equality..."

Such men and women learn from the "hard taskmaster of error" and want to be "left alone from government planning to grope for a plan of survival." They reject centralized control and shun bureaucracy. Farming communities are essentially classless and therefore are not plagued by strife between rich and poor. The farming mindset tends to eliminate both the arrogance of the wealthy and the indolence of the poor. The farming lifestyle cultivates virtue, promotes personal responsibility, fosters initiative and innovation, and instills a love of freedom.

Mini-factory practitioners are the new *georgoi*, the new freedom vanguard, those who will resurrect America from the ashes of aristocracy, the people "prerequisite to, the exemplar[s] for, democratic and egalitarian government." Such people think, act, and vote differently then either aristocrats or dependents—they do so as free men and women. They study the nature and anatomy of freedom and are actively engaged in its protection because they have the most to lose from the lack of it, as well as the most to gain from its thriving success. They cannot be duped by get-rich-quick schemes or political sophistry because they are intimately familiar with natural law. They scorn bailouts and handouts and ask only to be left alone by meddlers, however well-intentioned.

The health and longevity of Freedom Shifts are only equal to the education and virtue of their proponents. An abrupt change in America is unsustainable, and will be until enough people develop the mini-factory mindset through education and experience. The real battle for freedom is fought and won on the battlefield of perspective, rather than the streets of Washington. Political frameworks flow from cultural mindsets. First and foremost, the mini-factory model catalyzes this necessary shift in perspective.

There are those who point to the complexity of modern economics and our dependence upon commodities to assert that mini-factories will be ineffectual. As the argument goes, no matter what we do on a small scale, our core commodities will always be controlled by large institutions, which are owned by aristocrats, so mini-factories stop short of securing real freedom.

Understand that mini-factories can be as simple or sophisticated as their owners. They can be as simple as a family garden, or as sophisticated as an international investment firm.

Mini-factories can thrive in a complex economic environment. In this new model, education, innovation, and speed trump power, money, and size. Mini-factories are not necessarily quaint little family businesses naively operating on the low end of the economic food chain. They are any small, innovative, freedom-oriented organization or group that does anything more effectively than large, bureaucratic, aristocratic institutions. They drain power and privilege from the elite machine and spread them more equitably through voluntary means.

Also, keep in mind that there will always be things that can be done better by large institutions than by smaller entities, and, as I said, we will want these to stay. Still, a majority of the population operating mini-factories—with the accompanying mindset—can check and balance such institutions, and supply them with the cultural fabric wherein they operate best.

Others wonder how effective mini-factories can be in light of stifling regulation. That's the whole point. By creating mini-factories, we both produce individuals with a pro-innovation, pro-free enterprise mindset who will ease regulation through voting, as well as organizations that by nature fight misguided regulation. It creates a drip system as an antithesis to bureaucracy and faulty regulation—drop by drop, one individual and one organization at a time, the aristocratic system will be overwhelmed and deconstructed.

In our current model of government and corporate dependence, aristocratic institutions, laws and policies encounter only nominal resistance. More to the point, relatively few people are even aware of how burdensome our current regulatory environment is. Employees are largely shielded from red tape. Ironically, they feel its effects indirectly in almost every aspect of their lives, but few make the connection. Create a multitude of mini-factory owners and it's a different story. Suddenly, freedom issues are brought to the forefront as more and more people clash with bureaucracy, and mass consciousness is awakened.

Yes, it is difficult to operate a small business in the current political economic climate. Welcome to the Freedom Shift. Marginalizing the mini-factory model because of regulation is akin to saying that the American colonists shouldn't have thrown off British rule because it would have been difficult.

Yet another challenge is the economics of shifting from employeeship to a mini-factory, especially while balancing one's freedom education. I consistently encounter people who "get it," but struggle to implement the concept. With little or no savings to start a project, they're forced to work their job while striving to transition. In the meantime, they're trying to gain a real education and develop the skills needed to sustain a mini-factory.

Again, welcome to the Freedom Shift. I have no tips or techniques for making that transition easier. One can only ask if it's worth it. If it is, then do it. Pay the price. Bear that cross. Pay in time and effort and periodic setbacks and temporary failure what those before you have paid in blood. Give up frivolous TV and other forms of entertainment unworthy of your potential. Make it a family affair and invite family members to sacrifice with you to achieve a common goal. Do whatever it takes. Do it.

One of my former students didn't begin his freedom education until he was twenty-six, when he came to George Wythe University. Up to that time, he had never been an entrepreneur; he didn't think he was the "type." He worked full-time as a route driver with a local water delivery company while carrying a full class load and supporting a family.

After one year of attending the school, he began washing windows on the side to supplement his income. He quickly discovered that he could make money doing so, and that he could build a sustainable company. Four months later, he quit his job to build his window cleaning company, and has operated various mini-factories since then. After building his window company for a couple years, he sold it for a profit, then, through a series of events, became a freelance writer. Later, that developed into a successful marketing consulting firm, wherein he does business all across the nation from his home.

He and his wife homeschool their children, grow a garden, and are working toward owning a small family farm. In his words, he never would have thought this fundamental life shift to be possible just six short years ago. And, throughout the entire process, he has been dedicated to self-education, reading at least one book per week even after graduating from college. I am not suggesting this path for everyone, or for anyone, but rather that we all assess where we are and were we want to be, and make appropriate changes. My friend didn't go from route driver to best-selling author overnight; he made the difficult transition in small, punctuated leaps by always taking the right next step.

The reality is that most Baby Boomers and Gen-Xers must simultaneously gain their education while building mini-factories. In the absence of core Leadership Education in their youth, they must learn from the school of hard knocks. This means a few things: First, persistence is the key for those in this situation. If this is you, understand that you will fail. Get over it. Embrace failure as the price of education. Get up each time you fall and keep building, each time with more wisdom and strength. Secondly, understand that you truly need a depth education. Yes, it will be attained on a part-time basis, but it is vital. Engage with mentors. Read the classics. Consider distance studies at George Wythe University (www.gw.edu), the Center for Social Leadership (www.thesocialleader.com) or other similar institutions. And finally, take special care to raise your children to understand and embrace the mini-factory perspective, and help them get the education in their youth that you didn't get.

Understand that this choice between dependent employee-ship and independent mini-factories, between aristocracy and freedom, is not yours alone: Your choice in large part makes the choice for generations who follow. And your choice, though it may seem insignificant in the grand scheme, matters a great deal. As Buckminster Fuller said,

"Something hit me very hard once, thinking about what one little man could do. Think of the [ocean liner] Queen Mary– the whole ship goes by and then comes the rudder. And there's a tiny thing at the edge of the rudder called a trim tab. It's a miniature rudder. Just moving the little trim tab builds a low pressure that pulls the rudder around. Takes almost no effort at all. So I said that the little individual can be a trim tab. Society thinks it's going right by you, that it's left you altogether. But if you're doing dynamic things mentally, the fact is that you can just put your foot out like that and the whole big ship of state is going to go. So I said, call me a trim tab."

Every individual, every family, every team operating a freedom-oriented mini-factory is a trim tab. Each and every one is vital. Mini-factory owners are the new Founders engaged in the sustainable, bottom-up, inside-out Freedom Shift. Will you be among them or will you watch them on the sidelines? Will you choose aristocracy? Or freedom?

Coda

Freedom,

Are we witnessing your last breath, or coming rebirth?

Freedom,

Where are your friends now?

Freedom,

Why couldn't we face our fears and stand with you?

Oh, freedom,

You were everything...

Recommended Reading

Leadership Education is needed to promote freedom, establish and lead mini-factories, and improve a free society. The following readings were selected and are recommended because they address how to accomplish this:

*Tribes: We Need **You** to Lead Us* by Seth Godin

A practical, concise handbook for initiating, building, marketing and leading mini-factories, with particular focus on how to leverage technology in this effort.

The Global Achievement Gap by Tony Wagner

Includes the seven survival skills for the economy that schools should help every student develop, including critical thinking and problem-solving, collaboration across networks and leading by influence, agility and adaptability, initiative and entrepreneurialism, effective oral and written communication, accessing and analyzing information, curiosity and imagination.

A Whole New Mind by Daniel Pink

Discusses what schools need to teach to prepare students for success in the new economy, including the right use of right brain thinking, high concept thinking and high-touch leading; the ability to build projects like symphonies; and the skills of empathy, playing and meaning.

Five Minds for the Future by Howard Gardner

Gardner includes what he calls "the cognitive abilities that will command a premium in the years ahead." The five are: 1) mastery of the major fields (history, science, etc.) and at least one professional craft, 2) "ability to integrate ideas from different disciplines or spheres," 3) "capacity to uncover and clarify new problems, questions and phenomena," 4) respect and awareness of differences, and 5) understanding of the responsibilities to others.

Revolutionary Wealth by Alvin Toffler

Discusses what will create wealth and influence in the coming decades. Says schools should stop teaching rote memorization, fitting into standards, and obsolete job training and should start teaching individualization, independent and original thinking, creativity and "self-starting entrepreneurialism."

Future Files by Richard Watson

Argues that what is needed are creative, entrepreneurial thinkers. Left-brain proponents respond that this will just create techno-dependent artists. Watson's rebuttal is that we are already training up generations of expert-dependent followers when we need thinking, creative leaders and thinking, creative citizens.

A Thomas Jefferson Education by Oliver DeMille

An introduction to and overview of the philosophy and methodology of Leadership Education. Topics include the Phases of Learning and the 7 Keys of Great Teaching. The book also contains a graduated book list, discussion questions, and tips for getting started with Leadership Education.

Leadership Education by Oliver and Rachel DeMille

A hands-on how to book for parents, grandparents, non-traditional educators, teachers, mentors, and executives to educate for leadership, from infancy to grandparenting. It explains how to achieve the educational goals and ideas of the books listed above.

Mindset by John Naisbitt

Discusses major challenges ahead for leaders.

Additional Readings

The following works are also recommended for their relevance to the topics of aristocracy, technology, freedom and Leadership Education:

- Allan Bloom, *The Closing of the American Mind*

- Phillip Bobbitt, *Terror and Consent*

- Phillip Bobbit, *The Shield of Achilles*

- James Bryce, *The American Commonwealth*

- David Brooks, *Bobos in Paradise*

- David Brooks, *On Paradise Drive*

- Oliver and Rachel DeMille and Diann Jeppson, *A Thomas Jefferson Education Home Companion*

- Harry S. Dent, *The Great Depression Ahead*

- Harry S. Dent, *The Roaring 2000's*

- Ross Douthat, *Privilege*

- Rod Dreher, *Crunchy Cons*

- Barbara Ehrenreich, *This Land is Their Land*

- Thomas Frank, *What's Wrong With Kansas?*

- Thomas Frank, *The Wrecking Crew*

- Thomas Friedman, *Hot, Flat and Crowded*

- Thomas Friedman, *The Lexus and the Olive Tree*

- Thomas Friedman, *The World is Flat*

- Malcolm Gladwell, *Outliers*

- Alexander Hamilton, James Madison & John Jay, *The Federalist Papers*

- Victor Davis Hanson, *The Other Greeks: The Small Family Farm & the Agrarian Roots of Western Civilization*

- George Lakoff, *The Political Mind*

- Christopher Lasch, *Revolt of the Elites*

- Michael Novak, *The Spirit of Democratic Capitalism*

- W. Cleon Skousen, *The Five Thousand Year Leap*

- W. Cleon Skouson, *The Making of America*

- Thomas Sowell, *The Vision of the Anointed*

- William Strauss & Neil Howe, *The Fourth Turning*

- William Strauss and Neil Howe, *Generations*

- Alexis de Tocqueville, *Democracy in America*

- Michael Young, *Rise of the Meritocracy*

- Fareed Zakaria, *The Post-American World*

- Jonathan Zittrain, *The Future of the Internet*

Get Involved

Learn More & Purchase Copies of *The Coming Aristocracy*

To learn more about the principles and ideas discussed in *The Coming Aristocracy*, visit www.thecomingaristocracy.com and subscribe to the blog RSS feed. The website highlights existing mini-factories, explains the concept in greater detail, and provides practical tools, resources, and insights to help you build your mini-factory.

You may also purchase additional copies of the book on the website. Bulk discounts are available.

Engage With the Center for Social Leadership

The Center for Social Leadership (CSL) is a think tank and action organization dedicated to healing society, preserving freedom, and ensuring peace and prosperity for humanity. We empower ordinary citizens to make an extraordinary difference.

Humanity is experiencing dramatic changes. Traditional leadership is broken. Conventional human organization based on hierarchies and authority is outdated. Human consciousness is evolving. Technology has transformed the way we interact and enhanced our ability to have impact—for good or for ill.

To steer these changes, a new vision of leadership is needed. Not the old, hierarchical, positional, authoritative, privileged-elite leadership, but a new democratic, action-determined, service-oriented leadership. Through this "social leadership," mankind can achieve unprecedented happiness and fulfillment.

We invite you to engage with CSL by doing the following:

1. Download and read our free e-book, *Social Leadership: A Fresh Vision for Old Problems*, at www.thesocialleader.com.

2. Subscribe to our mailing list on the website.

3. Subscribe to our blog RSS feed.

Leadership Education Resources

TJEd.org

The official website of Thomas Jefferson Education.

Every person has inner genius. Thomas Jefferson Education consists of helping each student discover, develop and polish her genius. This is the essence and very definition of great education.

TJEd.org and its sister site TJEdOnline.com provide articles, videos and downloadable resources to help parents and teachers apply the 7 Keys of Great Teaching and the 4 Phases of Learning so your kids will love to learn, and you will inspire them and bring them face-to-face with greatness.

Other Works by Oliver DeMille

FreedomShift: 3 Choices to Reclaim America's Destiny

Americans who are so demonstrably willing to labor and sacrifice for the benefit of their posterity can only allow the destruction of the forms that protect our freedoms if they do not understand what freedom is, nor how to maintain it.

A FreedomShift is needed today; and to accomplish it, Oliver DeMille proposes The 3 Choices to Reclaim America's Destiny. Can it be possible that such a peaceful revolution can be accomplished by three simple choices made by a relative few?

A Thomas Jefferson Education:
Teaching a Generation of Leaders for the 21st Century

Is American education preparing the future leaders our nation needs, or merely struggling to teach basic literacy and job skills? Without leadership education, are we settling for an inadequate system that delivers educational, industrial, governmental and societal mediocrity? *A Thomas Jefferson Education* presents a new educational vision based on proven methods that really work! Teachers, students, parents, educators, legislators, leaders and everyone who cares about America's future must read this compelling book.

A Thomas Jefferson Education Home Companion

(with Rachel DeMille and Diann Jeppson)

This handy sequel has practical suggestions for helping children progress toward and succeed in scholar phase, including adult skills acquisition, how to conduct a successful family reading time, mentoring tips, club organization helps, how to create a "Momschool", etc.

Leadership Education: The Phases of Learning

(with Rachel DeMille)

This volume continues the Leadership Education Library with a survey of human development research that supports the TJEd philosophy and methodology, plus sections on each of the Phases of Learning: Core, Love of Learning, Transition to Scholar, Scholar and Depth. In addition, this book illuminates the adult phases of Mission and Impact, with a special Coda on Grandparenting. If you want to implement *Leadership Education* in your home, school, business or personal life, you will find this an invaluable tool. This inspirational book is considered by many to be the DeMille's best work.

Thomas Jefferson Education for Teens

(with Shanon Brooks)

This addition to the TJEd library is written to youth and adults wanting to accomplish a successful Scholar Phase—academics, personal development and mission preparation. It includes: "How to find the 'Real You'"; The Teen-100 List; How to study the classics; How to make the most of your mentor; Sample Simulations; …plus lots more!

The Student Whisperer

(with Tiffany Earl)

This book is designed to help you become a great mentor—a true Student Whisperer and leader at the highest level. It will also help you work effectively with such mentors as you pursue your goals and life mission. *The Student Whisperer* is part deep teaching of the vital principles of great Leadership Education, part self-help workshop, part example through parables, and part exploration of the great ideas that make mentoring and quality learning most effective at all ages.

Audios

The Four Lost American Ideals

In the hour-long recorded lecture, "The Four Lost American Ideals" Oliver DeMille draws from intensive study of the Founding generation to identify five defining ideals of Americanism: 1) Freedom, 2) Georgics, 3) Providence, 4) Liber and 5) Public Virtue. Although the first, Freedom, has not yet been fully lost, it is steadily declining because of the loss of the other four. These four ideals permeated early American society but have largely been forgotten.

The Freedom Crisis

Freedom lovers are losing, says DeMille, because they've been trained to think *sensus solum*. This type of thinking stifles creativity, inhibits innovation, creates cultural rigidity, and fails to sway the thinking populace. In order to conquer this ingrained challenge and win the battle for freedom, three things must occur: 1) Widespread *Sensus Plenior*, 2) Successful Innovators Building Effective Mini-Factories and 3) Statesmen & Stateswomen. Unless we can accomplish these goals, freedom will be lost for future generations. Absorb this 53-minute recorded speech to learn what these mean and how you can contribute to the solutions.

About the Author

Oliver DeMille is the author of *A Thomas Jefferson Education*, *FreedomShift* and other books, articles and audios on education and freedom. He is the founder and former president of George Wythe University, and a founding partner of the Center for Social Leadership.

Oliver is a popular keynote speaker, writer and business consultant. He is married to the former Rachel Pinegar. They have eight children.

Connect with Oliver on Facebook, Twitter and at www.OliverDeMille.com.